About the Author

PEOPLE-PLEASING, FAWNING, HEALING, SELF-LOVE, TRAUMA, SHAME, SHADOW WORK, RE-SILIENCE, BOUNDARIES – these are issues Annalie has been working through with her clients for the last twenty years as a trauma and performance coach. She has built an incredible network of champions and contacts that span Hollywood actors, billionaires, famous Premier League footballers, sportspeople and CEOs at the top of their game. Howling has worked with thousands of women to help them move through internal pain, triggers and difficult life experiences and into a chapter of their lives where they are no longer bound down by the past.

Annalie is known for her unique blend of Eye Movement Desensitisation and Reprocessing (EMDR) and coaching. Her corporate background enables her to apply EMDR techniques from that perspective rather than one of traditional therapy. She is a sought-after speaker and experienced facilitator, online and media commentator – she has run multiple sell-out retreats and live workshops across the world.

UNAPOLOGETIC

Unshackle Your Shame
Reclaim Your Power

Annalie Howling

First published in Great Britain in 2025 by Hodder Catalyst
An imprint of Hodder & Stoughton Limited
An Hachette UK company

The authorised representative in the EEA is Hachette Ireland, 8 Castlecourt
Centre, Dublin 15, D15 XTP3, Ireland (email: info@hbgi.ie)

1

Design by Goldust Design.

A CIP catalogue record for this title is available from the British Library

Hardback ISBN 9781399735995
Trade Paperback ISBN 9781399736008
ebook ISBN 9781399736039

Typeset in Garamond Pro by Hewer Text UK Ltd, Edinburgh
Printed and bound in Great Britain by Clays Ltd, Elcograf S.p.A.

Hodder & Stoughton policy is to use papers that are natural, renewable
and recyclable products and made from wood grown in sustainable
forests. The logging and manufacturing processes are expected to conform
to the environmental regulations of the country of origin.

Hodder & Stoughton Limited
Carmelite House
50 Victoria Embankment
London EC4Y 0DZ

www.hoddercatalyst.co.uk

For Amber, the anchor in my harbour

CONTENTS

ix Prologue: Wild Horses

1 Introduction: The Power of Shame

9 Unburdened
Shame and the trauma responses

23 Unmasked
Damaging behaviours and how we
turn shame in on ourselves

41 Unbroken
The worst moments and our limiting beliefs

61 Unstoppable
Shame, perfectionism and burnout

83 Unleashed
Reclaiming our sexuality

115 Unhidden
Shame at the hands of the medical establishment

127 Unchained
Relationships and break-ups

165 Unbowed
When friendships no longer serve us

181 Unapologetic
   A life without shame

203 Manifesto

205 Epilogue

209 Acknowledgements

211 References

PROLOGUE
WILD HORSES

Mustangs, the wild-living horses of the Western USA, have one natural predator: mountain lions. Like most animals, humans included, mustangs have an automatic programme hardwired into their physiology to keep them safe. When the horse senses danger, it knows that it must run. It cannot fight the mountain lion, so it does not try. Its overriding instinct is for flight.

To tame a wild mustang, you must first break it in. I know how this is done because, when I was attending an advanced trauma workshop for practitioners, one cold February morning in London, the lecturer showed us a video.

The garish light from the large projector screen filled the classroom. On the screen, a man dressed in denim, plaid shirt and boots entered the training ring, dragging behind him on a rope a wild, terrified creature. She was exquisite.

He walked to the middle of the ring while his assistant, a younger woman, closed off the only point of exit. He let go of the horse. She moved as far away as she could. But it could never be far enough.

The man then began bringing his whip down, long, languid strokes cracking the air, extending, flicking, cajoling.

The horse started to run. Danger.

Crack.

She ran faster.

The whip continued. It never touched the animal, but to the mustang, this alien, cracking tool of terror and the man wielding it were predators, threats to her life.

More loops of the ring.

We watched her stop and retrace her steps. Running the other way, she was once more at the beginning. No way out.

Eventually, she stopped. Frozen to the spot. I could see her eyes screaming. Her head dropped low.

A final crack of the whip.

She trotted over to her antagonist, head bowed.

'Good girl,' he said.

The video ended.

'And that is how you break in a wild mustang!' said the lecturer, seemingly delighted by this perfect illustration of the trauma response of 'fawn', the lesser-known fourth part of the fight–flight–freeze survival mechanism, inbuilt in living creatures to help us survive.

The wild mustang had run and run, around and around in the ring. She expected to outrun her predator, but she was trapped. Exhausted, she knew she could not keep running forever. As did the man who had decided to 'tame' her. So, facing the physicality of this predator that she didn't recognise, realising that there was no way out, she made a choice. The only choice that she had left. The only choice that might keep her alive.

Hanging her head in shame and submitting, she walked towards the thing she had believed would kill her in the hope that it might save her.

'Good girl.'

To make a wild mustang tame, first you break them.

The way to make a woman tame is to shame her.

How many times had I submitted to save myself?

Trapped.

Fawn.

Tame.

Shame.

I did not know before I saw that video how they tame wild horses.

But fuck me, did I know shame.

INTRODUCTION
THE POWER
OF SHAME

Every woman has felt shame. It is pushed on us. It gets everywhere. And it is insidious and sneaky. It masquerades as other things as it corrodes us from the inside.

Shame is hard to put into words; it is a felt sense that lies in wait for us in the shadows. Its power lies in its ability to convince us that our worth depends upon conforming to what others expect of us. When we don't, when we can't meet impossible standards set by others, it tells us that we are uniquely and irredeemably *wrong*, that our flaws are unforgivable.

The best way to keep a woman down is to shame her. When we feel like we are broken, we become isolated, we hide. Ashamed of our shame, deprived of our essence and our agency, we are compliant. We do not challenge the status quo. Shame is the last bastion of the patriarchy.

Shame comes out in people-pleasing, in the long lists of things we think we 'should' be or 'should' do to be acceptable to others. It's what makes us take what is offered to us, no matter how meagre, and accept it politely, prettily, without making a fuss. As women, we are taught to be 'good'. We are expected to put others' needs before our own and to earn love through service and self-sacrifice.

'Sorry,' we whisper in unison.

We are incessantly offered remedies for our anxieties and insecurities in the form of self-care rituals and personal development exercises. Sound baths, journalling, forest bathing . . . there's something new in the wellness space each week, it seems. Some of these things are useful for some of us, some of the time, while others just get added to our list of things we 'should' do (and don't). At best, they treat the symptoms and not the cause; at worst, when they don't work as promised, they simply provide more things to feel that we are failing at. They confirm to us that we are broken.

I believe that we urgently need something far more radical. These 'solutions' are a weak panacea at best: a cleansing ritual will not wash away a deep sense of shame that has been pushed onto us since childhood. A 'healing walk in nature' only gets us so far. What we need is to become a *force* of nature. The only way to completely free ourselves from the macabre puppet master of misery that is shame is to tear down the walls that have boxed us in and claim our power, unapologetically.

It's easy to offer compassion to others, to see their struggles and offer kindness. But turning that compassion inward, towards ourselves, is where the real work begins. It's about looking at our shame, our mistakes, our vulnerabilities, and saying, 'I see you. I accept you. And I love you anyway.'

This is the path to integrity. It's not about being perfect or having it all together. It's about being real, being honest with ourselves about who we are, what we want, and what we need. It's about letting go of the 'shoulds', the societal expectations, the pressures to conform, and stepping into our own truth.

Shame tells us we are too difficult, too broken, too unfixable, too unworthy and it's too late to change that. In this book, I want to show you why that is a lie.

I have to share this because every day, in the course of my work, I meet people who have been walking around with the pain of shame. Often for most of their lives. I have treated hundreds of people who lived their lives in the dark because shame told them to. People who have adopted an insufferable, impossible standard of perfection, trapping them in a people-pleasing cycle of self-persecution.

We do not have to live like this.

If people speak up about the real effects of their shame, I firmly believe that this helps others to end their suffering. So here you will find the stories of survivors, experts and professionals. And my story, too. As you read these pages, you will see what shame really is, what it does to us, and realise that you are not alone in your struggles, not the first to feel the sharp sting of shame.

I want you to find solace in the sisterhood of shared experiences, to meet others who have walked this path before you, so you can draw strength from their stories of resilience and triumph. This book tells our stories in a place where there is no shame.

I want us to break some of the rules we have unquestioningly been living our lives by, without asking who made these rules, why we follow them and what life would look and feel like without them. When we break these rules, we gain our freedom. We give ourselves the gift of authenticity and the power to transform not only our own lives but the world around us.

I need to tell you that some of the stories you are about to read, including my own, are often difficult and sometimes dark. They were difficult to hear, difficult to live, difficult to write. But difficult makes you who you are; laying these threads of our characters bare – in all their stunning, complicated glory without hiding – is liberation. Once that is done, we are free to reclaim our truth and find out what is available to us on the other side of shame.

Difficult gets shit done. Difficult is where the magic happens.

ABOUT ME

I'm a woman who lived with deep, entrenched shame for many years. I grew up in a household where I felt unsafe. I was told that the things that were done to me were my fault. As a child, I felt instinctively that this wasn't right, but of course I internalised the message all the same. As an adult, I took a corporate job in a competitive, masculine world. I did everything I felt I 'should' do to prove my 'worth' and, from the outside, no doubt I looked like a success. But it made me physically ill. It made me want to hurt myself, to claw at the mask that shame had made me wear. I was unfulfilled with no idea of my purpose, of what I truly desired. Even the idea of my own desire was lost to me. I tried everything – other than being myself, of course, because shame told me I was wrong and broken.

Eventually, inevitably, I burnt out. I'm divorced and a single parent. I've been through heartbreak, heartache, difficult situations and times when I felt totally lost. I am personally not grateful nor thankful for the things I have been subjected to in my life at the hands of others. But I accept that it all led me to where I am now. I place no more power in the hands of shame and I want you to feel this too.

A session with a friend who was a coach showed me that there was a different path available to me than the dead-end, dangerous one I was on. She inspired me and I soon realised what I wanted to do. At the time, the idea of leaving the comfort zone of my corporate life, no matter how harmful it was, to pursue a career in coaching seemed risky and 'out there'. This was a very new area, still seen as left-field and woo-woo in this country. But still, I moved to San Francisco, the city that was the home of this movement, and spent a few months doing all the courses I could to learn about trauma, about how we reach our potential and find fulfilment.

I now work with people from many industries and sectors, from Hollywood actors to elite athletes, from Olympians to 'corporate athletes' at the top of their game. I also work with individuals who come to me with deeply entrenched shame, with traumas in their pasts still obscuring their sense of self and clouding their understanding of what they really want.

I have never met anyone who does not have some kind of trauma. Male or female. Though women have a particular kind of shame received at the hands of the patriarchy, a system that still benefits from keeping us small and compliant. That means that there is no one that I have met who can't benefit from being released from shame.

I am often the first person to hear out loud what shame has been whispering to someone for years. In most of my sessions someone will say, 'I have never told anyone this before.' I refer to these intimate conversations as taking place in 'the house of no judgement' and the pages of this book are designed in the same way.

I live every day of my life now without any shame, with no fear and no apology. This allows me to be with my clients fully, no matter what they have been through. And I hope I can do the same for you within these pages. My biggest fear is not what someone will say to me; my biggest fear is that someone won't ever name their shame, their pain, their trauma, out loud at all.

I want this book to be a catalyst for deep and fundamental change in your life, in the way you see yourself at your best and the parts that you find harder to love, allowing you to accept all parts equally. I want you to leave here with hope, with faith in your own power, knowing that you do not have to live with shame any longer.

Are you sitting powerfully?

Then let us begin.

Some names have been changed to protect the innocent.

Some names have stayed the same.

Some names have been changed to give no platform to the guilty.

UNBURDENED

SHAME AND THE
TRAUMA RESPONSES

Something terrible happened to you. It was traumatic, but you don't know that at the time. Instead, when the shock subsides, you notice you have been given something.

It is a bag labelled 'Shame'.

Inside it there is a large, heavy, revolting, painful, nasty foe whom you must take with you wherever you go. It smells like shit, treats you like shit, and reminds you of how utterly shit you must be to have been given this bag. It tells you repeatedly that no one else has this shame. You are alone, disgusting, wrong and a failure.

When you are out and with people, you may be able to hide it somewhere. To do this, you must pretend that it's not there, you have no idea what it is and you have never seen it before. To deny its existence, you must also pretend to be someone that you are not.

But be warned, Shame will be pissed with this.

As a result, it will grow in size and magnitude later when you are alone. You may be able to get through the party without anyone seeing it, but it will still ruin your evening as you can hear it spluttering and muttering about what will happen later.

Your arms get tired, you physically cannot move anymore with the burden of Shame weighing on you so heavily. You have changed so many parts of yourself, worn masks and disguises, altered your behaviour, but Shame has not gone away. It has only become more powerful. So maybe you stop trying to leave the house. Perhaps Shame's narrative is so loud that you simply give in and lie on the couch next to Shame, letting it derail all areas of your life.

SHAME AND TRAUMA

Trauma takes parts of us, often in the most discreet of ways. Some trauma happens fast, too fast. It's a moment that changes everything. An accident, sudden, devastating news, an attack. Oftentimes, trauma happens slowly, seeping into our system over time. It can feel like misplacing something but you can't quite remember what it was, what it used to be, who you used to be.

I know that so many people are walking around with unhealed trauma, thinking they don't deserve to feel badly. This is the biggest paradox in trauma work: people don't feel worthy of the pain that they feel, and that to label it trauma would be to make an illegitimate claim.

But do you see? Shame wins again if not even your trauma is 'good' enough.

Whatever the experience was that activated a trauma response in your body, that went on to change how you feel about yourself, that is trauma. There is no bar to entry, no regulator that certifies trauma, no threshold an experience must cross to 'count'. If it traumatised you, that is trauma.

It's important to understand that shame and trauma are intrinsically linked. Shame is what's left in your body after trauma and it results in deeply internalised limiting self-beliefs.

Shame is, by its nature, shadowy and elusive, but we can understand it through 'I am' statements. These show how we turn the trauma back on ourselves:

He was cheating on me – 'I am stupid'
I watched as they drove away – 'I am unimportant'
Sexual assault – 'I am weak'
Eating disorder – 'I am disgusting'
Miscarriage – 'I am a failure'

We then treat ourselves in the way that these beliefs tell us we deserve to be treated.

'I am weak' – so I shall people-please and have no
boundaries
'I am unimportant' – so I will deny my needs
'I am disgusting' – so I will treat my body poorly

We are ashamed of our shame. If I believe I am disgusting, I don't want anyone else to know that. I want to try to mask that, to pretend that I am not, so that I am accepted. We all fundamentally fear rejection, so we bury our shame – our 'I am' beliefs – deeply so no one can see them. And here they fester, holding us back, making us apologise for who we are.

TRAUMA RESPONSES

Trauma responses are designed to keep us safe. They are activated to ensure we survive. We do not consciously choose what we do. It all happens far too fast for that. And yet, trauma responses leave us with shame.

Fight or flight. These are the two reactions to fear that are the easiest to understand. Stay and fight back or run away. But they are also often the least available options for women in situations in which there is any kind of physical threat from someone who is bigger than us, probably faster than us. Yet we often blame ourselves if we do not respond to a dangerous situation by fighting back or running away.

We blame ourselves if we flop, if we just pass out. Maybe even more if we freeze, rooted to the spot – which we later see as a lack of response, even though that *was* the response our brain chose. And possibly the hardest one for us to understand after the event is if we fawn. Fawning is when we find ourselves doing something to placate another. When we are in a place of danger it is often the aggressor, attacker or persecutor that we find ourselves appeasing. And we can hate ourselves for that.

FREEZE

One of my deepest shame statements that I had in my system came from an attempted burglary when I was in my early twenties. I was woken up at 5am one morning by my flat-mate's cat scratching. I realised it must be outside my first-floor bedroom window, on the roof, scratching to get in. So I pulled back my curtains and stood right in front of the sash window. There was a man standing on the other side of the pane of glass. It wasn't the cat – the scratching had been him trying to get my window open so he could get in.

I froze. I believed I didn't even make a noise. Though my flatmate ran in, so he must have heard something. He did all the things I wish I had but couldn't. He banged on the window, swore at him and, when the man took off, chased him down the street. To this day, I couldn't even tell you what the man looked like. I was so frozen that I can't even remember his face.

I didn't choose to freeze. My brain – specifically my amygdala, the part of the brain that takes over when it feels under threat – made this decision and my prefrontal cortex had no say in it. In these moments, your brain is taking in so much more information than you can possibly process consciously.

But I didn't understand that then. I feel deeply ashamed that I didn't fight or at least scream at him to fuck off or bang on the window or even run. It told me that I was helpless. That became my 'I am' statement. My limiting belief: I'm helpless and I am weak. So, if anything remotely frightening happens to me again, this is how I will react.

Imagine the relationships that I chose from this place, the work opportunities that I did or didn't take.

FAWN

Where a freeze response can give us the limiting belief that we are weak, the fawn response can make us feel we were responsible. That we encouraged the source of the trauma, that we brought it on ourselves. It is a common response for those who have suffered from domestic abuse, sexual assault and violence, bullying or even a narcissistic boss. And fawning is just as involuntary as every other response. We don't get to select it. And yet, I think we take on more shame from fawning than from anything else.

'But I did say yes to a drink with them.'

'I don't know why I would still reply to their messages after what happened.'

'Why did I kiss them / share an act of intimacy with them, after what they did?'

We do this because we are terrified.

I've never had a session yet when someone who tried to placate their assailant doesn't feel that they are in some way responsible. Even that they are 'sick' or 'broken' because they didn't fight back or run away. They too often refer to a 'grey area'. But this is a trauma response like all the others, selected by our brains when they decide that the other responses would not be suitable to guarantee our survival.

And there are no grey areas.

PEOPLE-PLEASING

People-pleasing and the fawn trauma response are not the same thing but they are bedfellows. People-pleasing can be a relative of the fawning trauma response, a way to cope. As a trauma response, fawning fires up before conscious thought and is motivated by survival. While people-pleasing is slightly more conscious and it comes from not wanting to be rejected.

People-pleasing guards against rejection. It is a way of hiding the things about ourselves that we think other people will find unacceptable. That we find shameful. It stops us from expressing who we really are and how we really feel. It makes us nod along compliantly. It takes away the word 'no' and puts it just out of reach.

NOT SAYING NO

How is it that we learn so early that many of the questions we are asked are in fact rhetorical? For us, at least. They are statements, really. They contain messages that are never said out loud but silently implied. They litter our daily lives. They arrive early into our family systems, and progress through into our work environments and relationships. They find us even in the most uncomfortable and vulnerable of times – in doctors' offices, during sex, when we are alone.

> **Do you mind if they watch the procedure?**
> **Can I sit here?**
> **You don't mind, do you?**
> **Was there anything else?**
> **Now that didn't hurt, did it?**
> **Does this feel okay for you?**

There is an answer that is expected by society, the patriarchy, by those posing the questions. A universal etiquette applies that tells us how the 'good girl' must answer. These non-questions support the structures of shame; what is being asked of us is subtle enough that we feel we still have the autonomy to decide our own fate.

Meanwhile, shame sits giggling in the background as we

are reminded, time and time again, that even when asked for our permission or opinion, for our time, for access to the most intimate parts of our body, we still do not have control.

'Silly girl,' shame whispers as the rug is pulled out from under our agency once more.

I have seen first-hand how shame corrodes someone's soul, which this quote below speaks to so tragically.

'SHAME IS A SOUL-EATING EMOTION.'

— CARL JUNG

THE GOOD GIRL

Being a 'good girl' means people-pleasing. It means denying your true essence for the sake of the comfort of others. But in doing this, we perpetuate these subconscious signals and systems that keep us inherently smaller than we are.

Shame-based rules and narratives constantly push for us to remain polite, quiet and adherent. They tell us that behaving in any way outside accepted norms of being a 'good girl' makes us a failure. These rules keep us separate even when we are together. Examples of 'good girls' are held up to us to demonstrate the mould of the compliant, unchallenging woman that we are supposed to fit into. This is phrased as a challenge as well as a reprimand, stirring the constant undercurrent of competition with one another.

To break the rules of being a 'good girl' is to transgress the boundaries placed upon us by the patriarchy and by each other. And that's exactly what we have to do. I want us to be able to find ways to express ourselves authentically and unapologetically – and if it means that I have to break rules that block my path, then I will proceed until I am apprehended.

Good is a block to life being as good as it gets.

Good is a limit.

Good is mediocre.

Good is lukewarm.

I politely decline. I do not want to be a good girl.

MAIA'S STORY

I got sober five years ago, when I was twenty-nine. I was a sex worker in my active addiction.

I spent ten years trying to get sober. I would go to meetings and I would hear people share about horrendous overdoses and I would think I wasn't 'bad' enough to be there. But I also wasn't good enough. So I just went out and did more.

We call it 'research': I hadn't tried all of the rock bottoms.

I lost my house and my job. I lost a relationship. I lost a baby. At one point, I tried to throw myself off a twenty-fourth-floor balcony. I have been in a lot of abusive relationships.

When I eventually got sober, I moved into a kind of recovery safe house for women and ended up going to a treatment centre for trauma for six months, which was harrowing and terrifying and brilliant and the best thing I've ever done. I'm still in the twelve-step recovery programme.

I feel a huge amount of sadness that I had so little respect for myself and put so little value on myself. But I didn't know any better. I can see now that I was looking for comfort. I also believe that I was raised in a culture that perpetuates the way that women are treated.

Shame tells you that you could have prevented what happened to you. That you walked into it and made bad decisions so it's your fault. I know that there are so many women out there who have suffered domestic violence for years and they talk to themselves with that same voice that I used.

The recovery from shame is not linear. I'm still learning to trust myself. I now have a role where I advocate for other people in the position I was in, but there is still a voice in my head that asks how I can possibly think I can do this when I was unable to advocate for myself?

One thing I know is that we need to keep saying, 'That happened to me too.' We need to keep sharing.

UNMASKED

DAMAGING BEHAVIOURS AND HOW WE TURN SHAME IN ON OURSELVES

That bag you carry with you is so heavy, it takes so much effort for you to lift it and hide it from the gaze of others that it distracts you from asking how so much shame got into the bag in the first place. It is clever like that.

'I am *your* shame,' it whispers. 'I am a part of you now because you are wrong. You are uniquely broken.'

Shame is so convincing that we fail to see how it circles around all of us, hovering in the air, waiting for its chance. We feed and nourish it, even in the way we speak to each other.

When we mean to express sympathy, we say: 'Oh, that's a shame.' Perhaps it's even 'a crying shame'.

When we call something out: 'Name and shame.'

In the way we talk about sex: 'The walk of shame.'

When we condemn: 'Shame on you!'

Or, like the mustang: 'You should hang your head in shame.'

SHAME ON YOU

Addiction, self-harm, eating disorders and negative relationships with our bodies are each a manifestation of the pain we carry, often in silence. Shame is a shadow that hides behind the masks we wear, distorting our sense of self and isolating us from the world. It feeds on silence and secrecy, convincing us that our struggles are unworthy of compassion and understanding. It so often drives us to seek solace in destructive behaviours or pushes us into patterns of self-sabotage.

People have long named 'aliveness' as the feeling they were chasing when they made a life choice that they later regretted. Cheating, addictions, even overworking and stress – all may generate that feeling of 'aliveness', of exhilaration and being wholly in the moment, for some of us. But, of course, this is not sustainable. We feel these moments as brief reprieves from inner pain and then we must go back to wearing our masks, now with even more shame to hide. If we lived in our authenticity, in our fullest shame-free expression, we would feel our natural aliveness in all that we do, in all that we are. We would not have to settle for snatched moments when we feel shame isn't watching, only to 'pay double' later for our perceived less-than-perfect behaviour or our harmful choices that we knowingly undertook in a moment of rebellion from the relentless pursuit of perfection.

These struggles are not merely symptoms of our individual shame and the pain that we carry but a reflection of a society that imposes impossible standards and stifles our ability to express our true selves.

For this is the hold that shame has: like a narcissist, it works to isolate us from the world around us. To live with shame is to feel as though you are trapped in a cave, looking out but never truly part of what is happening.

THE INNER CRITIC

When we spend our lives continually apologising for our authentic beings in order to save others from discomfort, we become uncomfortably numb. We become weary, we are made small, and that's when we surrender to the inner critic, the guard who enforces the rules and tells us what we are allowed to be. We put on masks to appear perfect and we say sorry every time we fall short of impossible benchmarks, hoping that we will be acceptable and accepted.

'They are judging you,' says the inner critic. 'You don't measure up.' Meanwhile, shame rubs its hands in glee. 'Saving face' is a rule that I had to learn to break. It's such a strange expression when you consider it. It's defined as meaning 'to keep your reputation and avoid others losing respect for you', the dictionary tells me. But where in this can we find respect for ourselves? People who may seek solace in addiction do so because they are trying to repair, as Mark Hyman so eloquently writes.

'ADDICTION HAPPENS FROM AN INJURY TO OUR SOUL.'
— MARK HYMAN

THE MASK

I stood in the shower, watching the blood pouring down my cheeks, dripping onto my chest. As I looked down at my fingers and nails, I heard an ever-familiar voice: 'What a fucking loser,' it sneered. 'Look at you. If people only knew what you were really like.'

'I'm sorry,' I whispered to my inner critic, who was always on hand in those days to remind me of my fuck-ups and failures. 'I won't do it again.'

But I would do it again. Again and again and again. For as long as I spent feeling 'less than' – an imposter in a life I did not deserve.

As the last of the blood washed away after another snatched moment of self-mutilation, the surge of shame immediately followed.

'You are pathetic,' said the voice. Landing that familiar blow.

'Yes,' I agreed. 'I am helpless, hopeless and weak.'

I am a failure.

After the nails scratched into my face, after the blood, after leaving the private cell of my shower, the cover-up began. Or continued. This wasn't just covering up my face, the marks, the scars, the open wounds with layers of make-up – though that took some time. No, this cover-up was far more detailed, designed to fool everyone into thinking I was 'perfect' and – the ultimate paradox – 'perfectly fine'.

My life was 'perfect': my beautiful daughter, my handsome, successful husband, the incredible home, luxurious holidays and savings for the future. But I was so deeply unhappy – or, according to my inner critic, 'ungrateful, unsatisfied and a fucking stupid bitch'.

This cover-up that I curated was the mask of perfection – and it was vital that it fitted just right. I wore and bore its weight beautifully, perfectly, all day, every day, until the moment came when I crawled into that shower, alone except for my vicious inner critic. That was when I entered a daze and clawed at that mask, trying to find the girl inside that I had once been. But this mask was one that could not be removed by brute force alone.

'I'm sorry,' I whispered out loud to the beautiful, empty, black-tiled room.

But there is another layer to this, the dirtiest secret of all, one that could not be scratched, clawed or washed away no matter how hard I tried: I was not sorry. I wanted the illicit relief and joy of the pain, the release of the silent scream that lived just below the surface of my skin, desperate to be let out.

I wanted to get out. I wanted to be free, I didn't want to be someone's wife. I didn't want to be a 'good girl', to be 'perfect' anymore, and this was the only place that I could admit that, even to myself.

I never felt the pain as I clawed at my face. That came after, when I looked in the mirror. The uneven, raw, hard-to-cover lack of discipline. How could I trust myself to make any decisions when I couldn't control myself, couldn't stop this, even when I promised again and again that I would? I couldn't even keep myself safe.

Of course, I didn't want the scars that I still bear now on my face, but for those moments, the briefest of moments when I slipped into a self-harm-based state of bliss, I felt two things: free and alive.

DR DAVID BROWN

Dr David Brown is a physician and a bariatric surgeon based in Idaho. I first discovered David's work when researching this book, via his YouTube channel. David's passion for his clients, the truth, and liberating people from deep, entrenched shame relating to their bodies stood out to me. In the US, where medicine is a commercial enterprise, David is unafraid to tell the truth, even when it goes against the popular view in his industry or does not help his business. I was interested in his perspective, as he deals with people every day who have spent many years battling their weight, internalising the shame that society heaps on people in larger bodies, who have reached a point where they have decided to have an expensive and involved operation.

Shame is a fundamental part of the personalities of everybody that I see in my practice. Bariatric surgeries are 98 per cent of what I do. Everybody who comes in the door feels ashamed and guilty. They feel like a failure for not being able to control their weight. I would argue it has been sort of programmed into their nervous system.

Why am I like this? Why can't I stop? What does it say about me? Why am I such a failure?

My highest goal for my patients is not just about their weight – it's for them to see themselves differently, to actually change their identity and what they perceive as their potential. In my experience, typically, women feel worse about themselves when they are struggling with their weight. They feel more shame relating to their body than men do.

During bariatric surgery, we staple the stomach, across little branches of the vagus nerve, which is a signalling mechanism and the largest nerve in the body, connecting the brain to the gut. It actually resets it, and so people's sense of smell and taste, as well as other things, are very different the day after surgery. It's also very likely to make the patient feel nauseous.

These effects are more pronounced in females. On the whole, men don't have much nausea after surgery. I joke that it's because men are more insensitive. Though I do think that women are, on the whole, either wired to or used to focusing on or perceiving their internal state.

A certain percentage of patients, maybe 3 per cent or so, will have persistent nausea and an inability to drink or swallow following bariatric surgery. They tend to all be young females. We do these tests to make sure there's nothing wrong with their oesophagus or stomach, there's no physiological reason for their symptoms, and almost always with these young women everything looks good. There is no reason we can find as to why this should be.

Ten years ago, this baffled me. I would say the field of bariatric surgeries was too dismissive of this and the attitude was simply 'give them the IV', as no one knew what else to do. However, I have come to understand that there is nothing wrong with these patients' stomachs or oesophagi – their symptoms are to do with shame and anxiety.

For many of my patients, the negative messaging they have received started at a very young age – not just in adolescence, but in infancy. They feel like their size limits their potential and all of them see themselves as 'less than' because of that. Many are carrying trauma that has been exacerbated by the way they have been subsequently treated. Often, doctors have told them that they should be able to lose weight, that they need more willpower and discipline – which, of course, drives the fundamental problem even more, as it makes them feel worse. I have heard horrible stories of patients' experiences with physicians and how condescending, arrogant and judgmental they have been.

Over the years, I've learned that you cannot predict who is going to do well after surgery in terms of achieving a healthy weight for them. In the past, my expectations for someone were clouded by my own prejudices. I'd think, 'This person won't do well, their life is chaotic, they come from a certain socio-economic background that means it's going to be tough for them . . .' These are actually so often the people who shock you. The greatest moments are when someone realises, 'I'm not who I thought I was. I am so much more.'

I have had several experiences when a woman comes in eight or nine months after surgery, and so much has changed for her. She tells me that, until the surgery, she never would have taken this risk to leave her unhappy marriage or apply for a certain job. And the key thing is that it's not because they've lost weight and they are physically smaller. It's not because they are suddenly being perceived as more attractive and getting attention. I think it's that their identity has been updated. Or rather, changed in a way that they have more authentic confidence in who they are.

Guilt and sadness diminish self-identity and self-esteem. If a woman stands in front of the mirror a year out from surgery and she sees the same person she did before the surgical intervention, to me, that means she hasn't been able to make the neurological changes to see more accurately what's actually there.

I had a patient who I operated on when she was seventy. About a year after her operation, she came in and, during our conversation, she broke down and she started crying. We talked and she told me the story of when she was living with her family on a small farm. Her father went out to the barn and got the trough for feeding the pigs. He brought it to the table and said to her: 'If you're going to eat like that, I'm just going to feed you like the pigs.' She was eight years old.

Over sixty years later, she was sobbing in my office about this. And she was a graceful, stoic woman. It was very, very clear that early events in her life had had a profound effect on her. It was beautiful to see her first recognise that and overcome it to some degree, to begin to let that go.

We need courage and bravery to be stronger than our shame, even if just for a moment to break free from it – that's why I love this quote from Brené Brown.

'OWNING OUR STORY CAN BE HARD BUT NOT NEARLY AS DIFFICULT AS SPENDING OUR LIVES RUNNING FROM IT.'

— BRENÉ BROWN, *THE GIFT OF IMPERFECTION*

RADICAL SELF-LOVE

The only thing that saved my face from my ritualised attacks every night was to stop apologising for who I thought I should be and instead become who I was always meant to be. It took time and so much self-compassion, but now I know that nothing is too shameful for us to unmask.

Radical self-love is the antidote to the poison of self-doubt. This is the place we are ultimately aiming for when we begin to understand that our worth is not determined by what others think of us, or what they are willing to give. It's not about external validation; it's about knowing, deep in our bones, that we are enough just as we are.

We will often do anything other than be alone with ourselves. It is rare that we are ever truly disconnected, thanks to our devices. Being alone is very different from being lonely. But to be happy with ourselves alone is the ultimate benchmark of radical self-love.

There was so much shame inside of me, so much stress, so much self-betrayal masked with make-up and platitudes and 'Yeah, I'm doing *great*! How are you?' that I settled for scraps, convinced that it was all I deserved.

But I know better now. I know that my worth is inherent; it is non-negotiable.

It's the act of reclaiming our power, of standing tall in our truth and of refusing to settle for anything less than what we deserve that shuts up the inner critic for good. And it is here where our true power resides, when the masks we wear fall away and we are left with nothing but our raw, unapologetic selves.

The job we have in front of us is to shed the layers of self-loathing that obscure our self-worth, keeping us trapped in cycles of self-destruction and disconnection. This is how we rise to the occasion, live our truth and love ourselves fiercely and unapologetically.

'"I'M SORRY"
THE TEAR THAT ESCAPED
"I'M SORRY"
THE SPACE I TOOK
"I'M SORRY"
WHEN I QUESTIONED
YOUR MOTIVES
"I'M SORRY"'

— ANNALIE HOWLING

EVA'S STORY

I was born in Eastern Russia in 1979, very close to the Chinese border. In those days, food shortages were normal and we regularly had to queue for staples like bread and milk. The city felt very cut off from the rest of the world and, as a child, I would disappear into the pages of a book. It was how I knew that there was a different life somewhere.

My mother started drinking when I was around eight or nine. I dreaded coming home from school as everything depended on her mood. This is when I started becoming a 'good girl', as I didn't want to cause or trigger anything because it would end up in punishment. Though, inside myself, I hated her.

My grandfather had been an officer in the army, and once a year before New Year we would receive a box containing special things like oranges, champagne, chocolates. One year, my parents hid the chocolates, in order to save them to take to a party. But I discovered the box of chocolates one day and, in secret, I started to eat them. One by one, putting the empty wrappers back in the box so it wasn't immediately obvious. I knew it was wrong but I wanted those chocolates so much.

Slowly but surely, I ate most of them. Then the time came for my parents to go to their friends' party. I knew I was going to be killed when they took out the box and realised that almost all the chocolates were gone. 'This is it, my last breath,' I remember thinking.

My mother gave me a huge beating because of this. She remembers it even now.

When I was a teenager, starting from about thirteen years old, my father would comment on my body. How I was curvy. He'd mention my breasts.

'Look at her body now!' he'd say in front of his friends. It was sexual in nature.

This was one of the hardest things to hear. I remember the comments and the men so vividly. It was like I had been stripped naked in front of thousands of people. I felt very unsafe and betrayed.

When I was younger, I'd believed I had a parent who gave me unconditional fatherly love. But then he changed. I suddenly felt alone against the world, like no one was going to protect me.

As a result of my father's sexualisation of me, I wanted to hide myself and never show my sexuality. Even to this day, it's hard for me to be sexual. I can never relax or let myself go. I had boyfriends and I later got married, but I always had this notion of what I should and shouldn't do. This is my biggest regret, that I was held in a straightjacket and could never let myself be this sexual woman.

For a long time, I didn't have any friends. Being lonely has been familiar to me throughout my whole life. I moved around a lot, starting from zero each time. I was so often alone on my birthday, alone on New Year's, just by myself all the time.

The only way I knew how to deal with the loneliness was by eating. Nothing gave me the same satisfaction. I'd shut down and, switching on the TV, surrounded by all the sweets I could get my hands on, I would spend the whole weekend alone doing that.

Binge-eating took over the majority of my life. It was like a worm in my head. I would choose it every time. Even on the occasions when I had other options, when I was invited out, I would spend my weekends binge eating. It was both my best and worst friend. I wouldn't even care if I had been judged, as the desire to binge was so strong. I looked forward to it.

Then, of course, there was also the vicious cycle. Because I was bingeing, I was gaining weight. So I thought I needed to lose weight to be acceptable. Only then would I be able to go out. 'I will start on Monday,' I would think, every weekend. And before I started, I needed to have a proper binge. It was my addiction, like a drug.

I am now in recovery. I am learning how to remove shame from my thoughts and my body, to treat myself with compassion so that I can finally heal.

UNBROKEN

THE WORST MOMENTS AND OUR LIMITING BELIEFS

'You made me do this.'

It doesn't feel like a fit. It's like a hand-me-down that you would never choose to wear but someone with a stronger voice is persuading you that it is the right thing for you.

'This is YOUR fault.'

The logic is off. The reasoning is faulty. You know this but still you begin to accept it.

Shame is sitting in the audience grinning, enjoying the action like it's a show. Shame's applause and cheers help you believe it. Over time, the screams from your mind and your soul fade and become silent.

We question ourselves, start to second-guess what was once our compass of clarity. Meanwhile, Shame nods vigorously – yes, we have got it wrong, yet again.

For all of the duplicities that we can endure, the most painful, confusing and wretched comes from the moment we surrender, like the mustang to its new master. The pain we receive from the hands of another is one thing – the blame we place on ourselves for allowing this is something else entirely. This may be Shame's greatest achievement.

But, meanwhile, the abuser wins. Shame keeps us captive for our newly crowned king.

This is how Shame behaves under the hypnotic rhythm of coercive abuse.

THE WORST MOMENT

When I work with a client, we focus on the 'worst moment', the one that haunts us, the one that changes the shape of our soul, the one that tells us to be anything but our authentic selves. The last moment with a parent at their hospice bedside, the last words exchanged with a loved one before they took their own life, the last 'no' that did not mean no to a predator.

It is not easy work but it's vital to find this trauma. And it so often lives physically in the body. Sometimes the client knows it's there, and sometimes they don't. We build up to this moment, but when someone is ready, I ask them to picture the scene, the image, the flashback to the worst moment.

The type of therapy I do with my clients is called eye-movement desensitisation and reprocessing (EMDR). It has a specific structure and focuses on locating and processing traumatic events, allowing you to work through them and move forward. It involves lateral eye movement – though sometimes this is done with sounds or tapping – while thinking about the memory of when the trauma was caused. The benefits are underscored by a wealth of clinical research. Over and over, I have seen it help clients release so much pain.

An important part of the process is a body scan. I help the person move through their body, like you would in a meditation. And then, wherever they find an area that is asking for their attention, I ask them to answer some questions with the first thing that comes to their head, without judgement. For example, if that feeling was a shape, what shape would it be? A cylinder, a triangle? Sometimes it's a rock or a ball. It might have a specific colour. It might be hot or cold. So often it is heavy and dark.

Eventually, we get to the crucial question we have to ask about how the trauma is showing up for them: 'What does that say about you?'

When I was training, I can recall being surprised at this question: 'What does that say about you?' We are unpacking people's most traumatic, vulnerable moments and this felt judgemental, shameful. But this is the point. And I know now, having received EMDR therapy a number of times, that when you reach this critical question, the answer is always there: the 'I am', the felt sense, the limiting belief that you have carried. This question provokes shame to place its sneer from deep in your system onto your lips. Then, once it is spoken, the spell of shame is, in part at least, broken.

LIMITING BELIEFS

We have to find the trauma as this is how we find the underlying limiting belief – the often-unconscious conviction that we have pushed down deep into our system. Limiting beliefs show up as shame statements: the 'I am' we talked about.

'I am a terrible person.'

'I am not good enough.'

'I am broken.'

Now imagine that this shame statement, which is rooted deep into your system, usually for many years, is the lens through which you view the world. This is the perspective from which you make your decisions and choices, the source of all the restrictions you place on yourself. Left unchallenged, this will always stop you living authentically as who you really are.

We need to acknowledge our own reality rather than present a sugar-coated version of ourselves to the world – I find these words on the next page by Sharon Blackie so helpful.

'TO CHANGE THE WORLD,
WE WOMEN NEED FIRST
TO CHANGE OURSELVES
– AND THEN WE NEED TO
CHANGE THE STORIES WE
TELL ABOUT WHO WE ARE.'

— SHARON BLACKIE, *IF WOMEN ROSE ROOTED*

I AM HELPLESS, HOPELESS AND WEAK

This was my limiting belief for so long. The foundation stones were laid in my childhood, and some later experiences – like the burglary I described earlier, and a car accident in which I think I just froze, feeling powerless – reinforced my shame statement. I was so determined to keep this 'truth' about me, as I believed it to be, hidden from absolutely everybody that I pursued perfection like an addiction.

I grew up in a household where I felt an atmosphere of collusion, which led to my exclusion and so I never felt safe. I learned quickly to fawn to try to keep my father happy. I internalised the message I was given – it was my fault when I felt hurt. It is the same old narrative: 'You made me do it.' I know that now. But as a child, you only have your own experiences to work from. You don't know any different. You are almost powerless to push back against what the adults are telling you.

As I grew up and went into adult life, even after I came to understand that what was done to me was wrong, that it cannot ever be a child's fault, I still carried the shame of the abuse in my body. I was helpless and weak because I 'allowed' it to happen; I must be bad to make people do that to me.

As limiting beliefs do for all of us, that deeply held and shameful conviction dictated to me the terms of how I would live. I avoided conflict. I was a people-pleaser. If I could appease, please and be liked – especially by men – perhaps that would compensate for my father's treatment of me? Perhaps it would quiet the limiting beliefs my inner critic chanted at me over and over again? If I could be a 'good girl', even for a while, I thought, maybe things would be 'normal', maybe I would be safe.

But that isn't how it works, of course. Listening to and acting on our limiting beliefs pushes us into a place of fear and shame and takes us further and further from the truth of our authentic selves. I know this now with an absolute clarity that returns me to my power.

The shame we hold in our body is so often not just a result of the trauma, but our reaction to what happened to us. The fear reaction of fawning doesn't just happen in extreme and dangerous situations; sometimes it's simply driven by a fundamental human need to be accepted. But when we see fawning for what it is – our body taking the decision to keep us safe, and not something we chose to do because we are weak – that is where self-compassion and healing starts.

GUILT VS SHAME

I am sometimes asked the difference between guilt and shame. Guilt is feeling bad about something you did or didn't do. 'I feel terrible I couldn't go to my friend's birthday, when I know she's had a tough year.' 'I'm so busy with work at the moment; I'm not spending enough time with the kids.' Sometimes guilt is there to show us that we didn't show up as the person we truly are and we need to make amends to put something right. Sometimes it is the result of the endless pressure put on us as women to live up to some ideal that we did not choose.

Guilt drags us down and steals moments of joy. It can be found in the endless rolling to-do list we all have scrolling through our heads at any given moment, a list that is impossible to ever complete. Guilt stops us being present in the moment as it holds us in the past and the future – *I shouldn't have done that; I really should do that tomorrow.*

But while guilt is corrosive, it is not the same as shame. Shame is that 'I am' statement we talked about; it becomes something you believe about yourself, rather than something that you feel bad that you did. 'I am a terrible friend.' 'I am a bad mother.' We tend to be able to share our guilt: 'Oh, I feel terrible – I forgot. I am so sorry.' Whereas we bury shame deep inside, terrified in case others find out that it is there.

PIA GRANJON

Pia is a complex trauma expert. Pia also is my therapist.

Pia has witnessed me and held me in a space safe enough to regurgitate the shame that I had repressed so deeply into my system over so many years. Never once have I felt judged in her presence.

I asked Pia if I could talk about our sessions here, breaking the tenet of client confidentiality, to lay bare some of her impressions of me in our earlier sessions, in the hope that showing the place I started from might help those just beginning or yet to begin a similar process.

Pia: Once you heal from what hurt you, you can understand the dynamic of your relationship with your primary caregivers and see each of them as individuals with their own personal history to carry. The pain can then change into more peace. Though, while we think about trauma as sexual abuse, emotional abuse, we know that the so-called 'little Ts' leave traces too. The trauma does not have to be at what we would consider the extreme end of the spectrum to create an impossibility to live with oneself as being worthy.

Annalie: I remember so clearly when you said to me: 'It's never been safe for you to relax.' That was one of the most astounding realisations you took me to. Growing up, my environment wasn't safe, and that had a huge impact – much wider than I had considered up until then.

Pia: I remember you had social varnish on your psyche and on your face – the make-up to cover your picking and the varnish of being beautiful and successful. What I was sensing was the heaviness of the pain and the fear that was hidden deep in that beautiful woman who was in front of me, but who was covering. At that point, any kind of relaxing, of letting go, felt dangerous to you.

Annalie: That epiphany – that clawing my own face was a silent scream – I had with you. It felt insane to have totally internalised such pain and not consciously realise why I was so driven to harm myself. I can't remember exactly what you said, but it was something like, isn't it ironic that you're scratching your face and that's what is facing the world? It took a long time for me to unpack and understand those behaviours. I pretty much had to start from scratch. I came to understand there was a voice in me. Like the Little Mermaid, there was something that I knew to be quiet under all these layers of things. That was what I needed to find, so I could listen and amplify it.

Pia: I always say there's a voice, a living voice. And part of the job of a trauma therapist is to just be there to say to the person, 'Can you hear the voice?' Because I can. So, can we welcome it in? How can we take care of it? We should not forget about the communication that our body gives to us, though we very often ignore it because of our education and our culture. When someone feels shame, they are not connected to others. They are connected to themselves, but in a negative sense. They cannot find peace. Like you, they cannot relax.

Annalie: That was probably the biggest piece of work for me. I stopped being afraid of being alone with myself. I had been lonely, but I learned the difference between being lonely and being happy alone by myself. I had to start sitting, being with myself alone, without stuff, without things, and now I crave that time with just myself. Finding peace was an important part of the process for me, of getting to the place where I know that I am lovable. That my self-worth comes from within.

'WOMEN AND GIRLS ARE GROOMED FROM BIRTH: TO BE KIND, TO BE POLITE, TO BE SECOND, TO BE A TARGET, TO BE A VICTIM.'

— PIA GRANJON

THE BODY KEEPS THE SCORE

I have been privileged enough to bear witness to many of my clients having the experience of locating the trauma in their bodies, identifying the shame and letting that shame leave their body. This is one way in which I know with such certainty that it is possible to free ourselves from shame and live unapologetically. It's not just my own experience – I have seen it happen again and again. It's an incredibly powerful and very physical thing.

It begins with self-compassion. Someone will get to the place where they can say, 'There's nothing that I could have done differently.' Perhaps they finally understand, 'I was only a child', or 'I didn't have the help I should have had.' Whatever the truth is that they need to be able to tell themselves, they find it. The shame no longer has a hold on them, and they can finally relax and let down their defences.

At this point, some clients tell me they feel nauseous. I have often seen people burst into tears but I have also seen them laugh. Which might sound really strange but there are many ways we can react when we begin to release shame.

The feeling in their body that the client identified as a physical presence usually begins to change shape at this point, as we do more rounds of EMDR – eye movement desensitisation and reprocessing. So a cold, grey rock that someone feels as heavy in the centre of their chest may become much lighter, moving up to the throat, and then be felt as a fog around their head.

What I find fascinating is that there is so often a connection between the original site of the heaviness, the pain in the body, and the way the trauma was experienced. I've had clients who have a bad hand or a wrist, and it turns out that was the hand that they were using to hold a loved one in their final moments. Or they feel a tension in one side of their face or jaw, which matches where they sat next to somebody in a car having a difficult or traumatic conversation. Someone whose overbearing parent would always have a controlling hand on their back will often feel the discomfort here.

When this trauma disperses, when the heaviness leaves, I can see people's entire faces relaxing. It's like seeing them without any mask, as they really are. Sometimes it looks like a weight has quite literally been lifted from them. Everyone is usually very tired afterwards. After I went through this process, I cried on and off for about two days, though I wasn't unhappy. It was just my system letting out what I had finally understood I needed to let go of. And from there on in, I never felt helpless, hopeless and weak again. I stopped believing that those limiting statements I had repeated over and over to myself were true of me.

CARA'S STORY

Cara comes from East Anglia. Her mother separated from Cara's father when Cara was young. Cara's mother worked a lot and it was important for her not to be reliant on anyone. A fiery matriarch of the house. 'You could knock a lamp off a table – it could have been "Don't worry", or you would be seeing stars, it was that fractious,' Cara recalls.

Cara is a pseudonym, but this is her real story. She lived under the control of shame for forty years. She has found a purpose in sharing her story: the power of naming shame in safe spaces.

He was a martial arts teacher who came to do after-school clubs and would take kids swimming. A boy had made an accusation about him but no one listened.

He asked my mum if he could take me and my friend swimming one Saturday and my mum said yes. At that time, this wasn't usual. I was only ten. I remember that my sister didn't want me to go.

It started in the pool – touching, hugging, grabbing. I felt uncomfortable, deeply uneasy. Then it progressed. He took us to the bathroom and my friend and I had to take turns being touched while the other looked on. I was a people-pleaser, even then. I kept telling my friend not to worry, even though I was so worried.

He took us back to his house and put porn on the TV. Not that I understood what that was. I didn't understand at all what was happening.

I remember being upstairs and a horrible brown towel in the bathroom. I looked at the tiny bathroom window, wondering if I could get out. But of course there was no escape. I grew up around the time of the Moors murders. I knew what had happened to those children and I really thought I was going to die.

He had penetrative sex with me in his bedroom. My mind was trying so hard to protect me.

He dropped me back to my house.

My sister was the first to realise that something was wrong with me. When my mother started to understand what had happened to me, she started screaming.

The police arrived and the detective was the father of my friend from school. My mother couldn't cope. Her hysteria was the most awful moment.

That's when the shame hit. I never wanted to be in a position like this again, with all of these eyes on me.

The detective told me, 'Paedophiles pick their victims because they are meek and mild.' In that moment, it informed me of who I was. I then perpetually had that confirmed to me by my mother and my sister: 'You are the weak one.' I came to believe that 'bad things happen to people who don't have value.'

After that day, what happened to me was never discussed again. In my teenage years, if something came on the TV when we were all sitting there, nothing was ever said but you could have cut the atmosphere with a knife.

*   *   *

Sometimes, following this attack, when Cara's mother's mood darkened, she would strip Cara and her sister naked and force them out onto the residential street where they lived. Neighbours, peers, strangers, men could look at their naked, adolescent bodies standing frightened in the street.

As she went into adulthood, Cara was a trailblazer in her career, succeeding in major corporate roles. However, her drive and motivation came from an addiction to work and success. Now she sees that 'I needed to be valued because I never had it from myself or people around me . . . I don't think I would have had half the amount of success if I hadn't had that horrific sexual attack, and my mother hadn't beaten me and made me feel like shit. It gave me that drive to prove them wrong and prove something to myself.'

Cara lived with shame for forty years. She describes herself as trying to craft a 'perfect' adult life to hide how she saw herself: 'worthless'. People-pleasing became her portal of protection. Like so many victims, she built layers to cover and hide the big shameful secret. Meanwhile, the void between her outward success and her internal world became ever bigger and darker.

Cara always knew that she was gay: 'I knew before what happened that I liked girls. Though my mother weaponised it and used it to demean me throughout my whole early adulthood. "Look at those queers over there," followed by, "not aimed at you, darling," which was total bullshit. I knew it was aimed at me.'

There is a damaging and ignorant assumption sometimes made of victims of sexual assault who may identify as

LGBTQ+ that they are 'only gay because of what has happened to them'. This had been levelled at Cara. 'I always found that really difficult to accept,' Cara explained. 'It devalued my decision about who I was.'

There are forums full of people who have been attacked and haven't come out, and not because they are afraid of being judged or rejected, but because following the 'shame' of the abuse they fear that another dynamic, another shift in narrative taking up more space, is too much for their families to bear. Or they fear the attention they feel will be on them. This is an extreme act of people-pleasing that places the perceived needs of others above our own authenticity and identity.

'YOU ARE NOT RESPONSIBLE
FOR THE ACTIONS OF
OTHERS. IT IS THEIR SHAME
TO CARRY. IT IS NOTHING
TO DO WITH YOU. SPEAK IT
OUT LOUD TO YOURSELF
IN FRONT OF THE MIRROR.
ACKNOWLEDGE IT, FEEL
SAD AND ANGRY THAT IT
HAPPENED. KNOW THAT
YOU DON'T NEED TO FEEL
SHAME. IT'S NOT YOUR
SHAME. IF YOU CAN'T SPEAK
OF IT TO PEOPLE CLOSE
TO YOU, FIND A FORUM
AND SPEAK IT THERE FOR
THE FIRST TIME. YOU ARE
NOT THE ONLY ONE.'

— CARA

UNSTOPPABLE

SHAME, PERFECTIONISM
AND BURNOUT

The doorbell rings again.

I'm not ready. I had said that I wasn't ready, that this isn't a good time. I have been keeping so busy, occupying my time with the list of tasks that spools on and on. I can't let my guard down tonight.

A knock this time. I can sense him standing outside my door. His energy begins to seep under the gap, filling the space around me.

I want to call somebody. I haven't been speaking to my friends so much recently. And when I did, they all told me the same thing: that I had to face him. I couldn't shut him out, pretend he doesn't exist. It is the only way to heal.

They don't understand, they have been with him since the beginning, welcoming him in, seemingly with open arms, having him over at any time of day or night. They would even post about him, sharing photos of tear-filled reunions with him. All of a sudden, it seemed he was everyone's mutual friend.

I had long since turned off my notifications.

'Please, I can't do this now, I don't have the strength in me.' I try to reason with him from the other side of the door. 'I have been doing everything perfectly. I have been keeping it all together. He said that as long as I did that, you wouldn't come.'

'Who told you that?' he enquires, not unkindly.

'Shame,' I answer.

Shame looks up from the sofa as I say his name. We had been close before but mainly I saw him at parties and work. And at our regular 'morning after the night before' check-ins, when I am hungover and tired, and we rake through the previous evenings to find times I'd done or said the wrong thing. But now, since it happened, Shame is never far away from me.

'That's not how it works,' he explains. 'I can open the door, I have a key, but it would be better if you would just let me in. I'm afraid it doesn't matter to me if you've done the laundry, sent thank-you cards, remembered birthdays or got around to painting the scuff on the wall where you pulled that picture down the last time I tried to see you. We need to talk tonight.'

Panic begins to rise in me. I have been fine doing things my way. I don't want him here. I have done so well at keeping him out. I am afraid of him. Afraid of what he would see. Afraid of what I will see in myself.

The lock clicks and the door opens slowly. I raise my eyes to look at him.

'Won't you invite me in?' he asks, hopefully.

He is big, but not as big as I had remembered him to be. There is something oddly familiar about him now, almost comforting. He places the box in his arms onto the floor. Then he begins, as I feared he would, with the truth.

'I am not going to say that this won't hurt you,' he says. 'It will be painful and we might have to have this conversation more than once. But I can assure you, this is less harmful than the endurance test that you are currently putting yourself through day after day. I can see how tired you are.'

'I'm so scared that if we have this conversation now I will never recover,' I blurt out. This is the most honest I have been since it happened. 'If I have to face the feelings and thoughts and look through that archive box of memories that you have brought me, I worry that I won't ever be able to get back up again.'

'I understand, but I still think you need to look in the box.'

I am too tired to fight any more. The energy I found to complete all the tasks that shame gave me, to present myself perfectly to the world to prove that I am not falling apart, seems to have disappeared. So I look at the items in the box he has brought me. The stories behind each one flash across my whole body like I am trapped between a projector and a screen. The pain comes then. The searing, swelling, burning, crashing pain. The expansive hole in my chest. It's getting bigger and louder, burst after burst, like a fireworks display I never wanted a ticket for.

'I can't do this,' I cry, looking him dead in the eyes.

'You have to,' he says. 'I am going nowhere.'

I think I black out eventually. I don't remember how it ended. But when I wake up, my heart rate is much calmer. I notice the light outside my window is a different colour and I feel a sensation of something new. We are both slumped on the floor.

'It's within you now,' he says, 'so you can stop running from it. It will still hurt, maybe forever, but you will be able to cope with it. Much better than you thought you would.' He stands to leave.

'Where is Shame?' I ask, realising my codependent, ever-present companion is nowhere to be seen.

'He left,' Grief answered. 'You do not need him anymore.'

PERFECT

Be the perfect employee, partner, parent, friend. Please others at all costs. Do not disappoint. Strive and keep striving. Don't stop, even though you are exhausted. Even though you don't know who you are and what you want any more. Keep going, even when you think you might be losing yourself.

These are the instructions coded into what we are told womanhood is. Often, the result is that we become so consumed by meeting everyone else's expectations that we forget to attend to our own needs, driving ourselves to burnout. The exhaustion that follows isn't just physical; it's an emotional and spiritual depletion, a by-product of the shame we carry for not being able to do it all.

Deeply ingrained patterns of self-sacrifice lead us to neglect our well-being in the name of perfection. The noise of society's expectations drowns out our inner voice, which is trying to tell us who we truly are and what we want our lives to be. The quest for perfection is a trap set by shame – a trap that drains us of our vitality and joy, our unapologetic expression.

When terrible things happen – when we lose people who are important to us, for example – we can still hold onto this need to appear perfect, together, like we have got this. Shame tells us not to show ourselves as we really are in those moments: devastated, afraid, in pain. Instead, it demands that we hold onto that mirage of perfection. But it doesn't work. We cannot dodge grief. And we cannot allow shame to tell us otherwise or we will never heal.

In no situation can we be authentically ourselves if we are trying to contort ourselves into shapes decided by others, by shame. We cannot follow our own path if we are relying on signposts sending us down the conventional, safe path.

To break free of the toxic relationship between shame and people-pleasing, which leads to burnout, we must unlearn the habits and beliefs that keep us trapped.

'IF YOU LOOK FOR PERFECTION, YOU'LL NEVER BE CONTENT.'

— LEO TOLSTOY, *ANNA KARENINA*

BURNOUT

When I was twenty-nine, I suffered a catastrophic physical and mental burnout.

By that point in my life, I had been sprinting my own personal marathon for years, ignoring every finish line, white-knuckling through qualifications, masters degrees and accolades in the hope that these external validations would somehow fill the crevasse of emptiness inside of me. On the outside, I appeared to be doing brilliantly. Inside, though, pieces of me were falling off.

I understand now that my perpetual need for performance was me trying desperately to make myself invulnerable. I had learned early on that vulnerability was a weakness. Growing up in a violent home, I'd had to protect myself.

My first job in construction, a male-dominated, hyper-masculine industry, only reinforced that lesson. I armoured up. I repressed my femininity, refused to cry and pretended to be 'as tough as any man'. Understanding trauma and shame as I do now, I see that this industry, where toxic masculinity was rife, was the perfect setting for me to be repeatedly triggered and fawn my way through my career, frightened, fearful, faking.

The hours, travel, conditions and environments were unrelenting and unforgiving. This was also a time before the #MeToo movement. I was touched, grabbed, groped, criticised and my body commented on publicly. I was harassed and told often and in no uncertain terms that being myself was never good enough. I was instructed to 'keep the client happy', like a performing corporate courtesan. 'Wear a pretty dress,' said my boss. 'Stay out as long as the client wants to.' It didn't matter how many 3am finishes I accumulated in a week, I was expected to be at my desk at 8am every morning.

I wasn't living in alignment with my true self and it was killing me. My relationships, both personal and professional, suffered because I wasn't showing up authentically. I was too busy trying to be someone I wasn't – someone who couldn't be hurt, who didn't need help. While the real truth was that I was hanging on by a thread.

My drive to succeed, to be financially secure, was actually a need to never return to the instability of my childhood – an attempt to outrun my past. But, instead, I was running myself into the ground.

When I reached the state of full burnout, it pulled me out of my flaw-covering perfectionism with such velocity that it seemingly came from nowhere. I was constantly exhausted, ill and experiencing a suffocating sadness. I had successfully ignored all the warning signs, so burnout did what it does best: it floored me physically. It even threw me off my constant pursuit of people-pleasing.

I was unwell in every sense, yet I couldn't understand why. I had tests, reset breaks at health retreats and holidays. Yet I never returned renewed. I had symptoms of IBS which made me anxious every day. I had every intolerance test imaginable, thinking I could just cut out a food group. They all came back clear.

I was not intolerant to dairy or gluten.

I was intolerant to my life.

This was the elephant in the room; this was the thing that, no matter how perfectly I tried to sweep it under the rug, still grew. I was in a role that was so far out of alignment with my soul that my body was going to show me my own personal path to my 'why'.

RADHIKA DAS

Radhika Das is a globally renowned Bhakti yoga practitioner who practises the ancient practice of kirtan – a call-and-response musical meditation dating back more than 5,000 years that can be practised by anyone. Radhika and I first meet during a recording of his podcast, For Soul's Sake.

As we journey through life, our perspective changes. In our youth, we're consumed with how others see us. By middle age, we begin to realise that other people's opinions hold little weight. And as we grow older, we understand that most people weren't thinking about us at all. This revelation can be both freeing and humbling, allowing us to focus on what truly matters.

My first encounter with this truth came during a kirtan experience in Spain. I was sitting in the back of the room, overwhelmed with a personal crisis. My partner, back in the UK, had just sent me a message saying our relationship was over. Desperate and disconnected, I was furiously trying to get a response, but the lack of signal left me isolated and anxious. Meanwhile, the room was alive with joy – people singing, dancing, and connecting in a way that felt completely out of reach for me in that moment.

But something shifted. I decided to let go of my frustration and just immerse myself in the experience. I started dancing, chanting, and soon found myself swept up in a wave of euphoria. The sadness and anger that had gripped me began to dissolve. At the end of the session, I approached the swami leading the kirtan and asked, 'What was that? How did you create this space where all my pain just disappeared?' We talked for hours afterwards, a conversation that left me with a deep sense of warmth and positivity about my life again.

There's a powerful analogy often used in spiritual circles: digging for water. We are like people standing on the surface while water, representing spiritual truth, is deep underground. Instead of digging deeply in one spot, we often move from place to place, trying a bit of this and a bit of that – some chanting here, a yoga session there, maybe even consulting a medium or trying crystals. The truth is, if we persist in one path, eventually we will reach that water. But to do so, we need to commit to one direction and trust that the walls are getting moist as we dig deeper.

Shame is a powerful force. It can shatter our sense of self, leaving us feeling isolated and unworthy. Yet, the purpose of these moments isn't to diminish us but to cultivate humility within us – a humility that doesn't require us to think less of ourselves but to understand our place within the broader tapestry of existence.

Humility isn't about self-deprecation or dwelling on our perceived shortcomings. It's not about telling ourselves that we're worthless for indulging in vices or failing to grasp spiritual truths. True humility is something deeper. It's the recognition that life is more than what we accumulate. It's about how we serve, love, and connect with others. While we may work hard to build a life through acquiring things, it's through giving and sharing that we truly create a life worth living.

Often, in our pursuit of material success, we end up doing things not for our own satisfaction, but to please others who may not even care. Living a 'normal' life often means conforming to the values of a world gone mad, where true happiness and authenticity are sacrificed on the altar of societal expectations. Sometimes, it's better to be seen as unconventional so that we can live in alignment with our own values, even if that means stepping outside the boundaries of what's considered normal.

The struggle often comes from our obsession with perfection. We live in a world that celebrates perfection over progress, leading to feelings of inadequacy and depression. But what is perfection? It's an illusion, a standard set by a society that often values appearance over substance. In my work, I've met some of the wealthiest people on the planet. Despite their material success, they often struggle with the same feelings of inadequacy and disconnection that plague the rest of us.

There is a profound peace in simplicity. In a culture obsessed with accumulation – whether it's practices, possessions or achievements – the answer might lie in stripping things down to the basics. What do we truly want? What is the essence of our life's goal? Sometimes, the most powerful step we can take is the simplest one.

Life will test us. We all experience moments when our spiritual practices feel dry and unfulfilling, when we question the very path we're on. During these times, one safety net is whatever keeps us connected to ourselves and our purpose. The second net is philosophy, which helps us rationalise and stay patient. But the final, most reliable net is the community of those intoxicated with divine love. Surrounding ourselves with these souls can lift us when we're at our lowest, reminding us that we are not alone.

Real happiness is not something external. It's something we feel when we come across a genuine spiritual path, a warmth that radiates from within. But the illusion that happiness is tied to material success or societal approval often clouds our vision. We start to believe that we can't be happy unless we've achieved certain external milestones – or worse, that suffering is a necessary prerequisite for joy.

Living authentically means aligning our lives with our values, whatever they may be, and staying true to them, even when it's hard. There's also a beauty in that shared humanity, a reminder that we are all on this journey together.

INTEGRITY

When you consistently try to outrun your trauma, grief and suffering, you can indeed keep up the race for a while, as shame stands there in its coach's uniform, goading, sneering and threatening. But never cheering you on.

But the score is being stored by your system. *I can do one more lap*, you think. *Win one more medal, get one more score on the board.*

Until you can't. Until the metaphorical wheels literally come off.

The turning point came when I was forced to confront the reality that my life was a shambles. My relationship with my true self and with my integrity was, to put it bluntly, non-existent. My integrity was shattered – not by some grand act of betrayal, but by the small, everyday lies I told myself to survive. This realisation marked the beginning of a profound transformation, but it wasn't easy.

A lack of integrity is often a survival response, born out of a deep-seated belief that it's not safe to be vulnerable. For years, I had armoured up to protect myself, to be accepted, to feel loved. Letting go of those layers felt like stepping into the unknown. But it was necessary.

Sometimes, my mind would feel like it was wandering, presenting me with an alternative life. At the time, while I was in the middle of burnout, believing my body was betraying me, I saw those 'visions' as nothing more than indulgent daydreams, a self-indulgence distracting me from what I should have been doing.

I know now that was my intuition, calling me home. Bringing me back to my integrity.

My intuition had been given a back seat in pretty much all the decision-making I had done up until that point in my life, so that, by then, I could barely hear her call. She was so used to being silenced by shame, to being undermined by the inner critic. Meanwhile, my vulnerability was something that I policed and pushed so far inside of me that it never saw daylight.

We throw around the word 'integrity' a lot but we rarely talk about what it really means. It's not just about being truthful; it's about being consistent. Integrity is not a one-time act, it's a habit, a way of living consistently, day in and day out. If someone regularly tells you one thing and does another, they are showing you their lack of integrity.

Following my burnout, I learned that integrity is not a destination. It's a journey – one that requires constant vigilance and a commitment to vulnerability. It's easier, even now, to slip back into my old patterns, to armour up, to close off. But I know that to live in integrity means to consciously choose vulnerability, even when it's uncomfortable, even when it feels like the last thing I want to do.

When I began to rebuild my life, I had to start with the basics. I had to ask myself: where am I out of alignment? Where am I not being true to myself? It was a painful process, but also a liberating one. I learned to say no when I meant no, to stop people-pleasing, and to honour my own needs. Every time I chose to stand in my truth, I was reclaiming a piece of my integrity.

The only way to do this is to accept and even embrace imperfection. Self-compassion is also vital if we are to allow ourselves to let go of the need to please others at the expense of our own health. Questioning the standards we've always accepted without question can feel like a huge task, but it is also an invitation to embrace a life where we prioritise our own well-being, redefine success on our own terms, and break free from the burnout that comes from living in shame.

Declaring sovereignty over your own story is a testament to the power of self-love and acceptance in a world that thrives on judgement and conformity.

Anxiety thrives on creating chaos in our mind and body by pushing us away from who we are at our core and into who we feel that we should be. Peace begins the moment that we accept our whole self, unapologetically. These words on the next page by Bessel van der Kolk really speak to me.

'AS LONG AS YOU KEEP SECRETS AND SUPPRESS INFORMATION, YOU ARE FUNDAMENTALLY AT WAR WITH YOURSELF.'

— BESSEL VAN DER KOLK, *THE BODY KEEPS THE SCORE*

GEMMA RICHARDS CALDER'S STORY

I never set out to be a make-up artist. In fact, I didn't even know what it entailed. But I've always been an artist. I spent years studying fine art in Bristol, eventually moving to London, where I had a studio in Wimbledon. I painted and I exhibited and sold my work at the Chelsea Langton Street Gallery.

I loved painting. It was my therapy, my joy. When I painted what I wanted, it felt freeing, authentic. But then, suddenly, my art was no longer mine. It was vulnerable, exposed in galleries, waiting for judgement. Would someone buy it or would it just sit there, dismissed and unseen? It was stressful – my heart out on display, my livelihood hanging by a thread.

Then there were the commissions – pieces I had to create to order. I had to sell to survive, but each sale felt like a transaction for my soul. The more I painted for others, the more I felt disconnected from the very thing that once brought me peace. Art became a source of pressure rather than passion; the love drained out of it when it was more about survival. I felt like I was losing myself.

I stopped painting entirely after that. It was distressing. In my early twenties, I was adrift. One day, I helped a friend with a low-budget film, working in the art department. There, I met a make-up artist who was creating a black eye on an actor. I was fascinated. Watching her work, it clicked – this was something I could do, something that married my creativity with a tangible skill. For the first time, I saw a path that felt right.

I took out a loan and enrolled at the Delamar Academy in London, where I learned the art of make-up. My background in fine art allowed me to take the shorter course, just four months. I also trained in hairdressing because I wanted to focus on film, not fashion. Fashion was never my world. My sister was a model and I saw first-hand the toll it took on her. It's a world far harsher than acting, one obsessed with appearances and unforgiving of flaws. I never wanted to be a part of that. In film, there's more room for expression, for movement, for life. I needed that freedom.

That decision changed everything.

Make-up artistry became my new canvas. It was a completely different experience: social, connected, vibrant. I wasn't alone in a studio anymore, I was part of something bigger, working with others, creating art on faces instead of canvases. It was dynamic and interactive, and I thrived on it. There was still beauty in what I did, but now it was shared with others, alive in the moment, not hanging silently on a wall.

Some people might have thought I was throwing away a dream when I gave up art. But, to me, it was liberation. My family, especially my sister, supported me fully. She believed in my need to change course, to find something that made me truly happy. And that's what this new path gave me – a chance to be happy, to create, and to be part of something that felt true to who I was.

Looking back, every step, every detour has its purpose. Nothing is wasted. It all led me to where I am now, and I carry those lessons with me every day. Make-up artistry is my passion because it allows me to be who I am – creative, connected and in love with what I do. It's a beautiful thing to wake up excited to go to work, to transform someone with a brushstroke, to bring a character to life, to make someone feel beautiful or fearsome.

There's something incredibly powerful about being part of someone's transformation, about seeing them step into a role, become someone else. It's like a switch flips and they're no longer themselves. But underneath it all, they're still human, still carrying their insecurities and fears. My job is to help them bridge that gap, to make them feel ready to face the camera, to be their best self in that moment.

In this line of work, you get to know people deeply. You're there when they're vulnerable, when the mask is off – literally and figuratively. The bond we form is like family, forged in the long hours, on the night shoots, through the shared exhaustion and the triumphs of a job well done. We're creating something magical, and that's a bond that's hard to explain to anyone on the outside.

In the end, what I've learned is this: beauty is about feeling comfortable in your own skin, about owning who you are, flaws and all. It's not about perfection. It's about authenticity. The most beautiful people are the ones who are unafraid to be themselves. That's what I try to bring out in everyone I work with – the confidence to be who they are, both on and off the screen.

UNLEASHED

RECLAIMING OUR SEXUALITY

'Hygiene strip – item cannot be returned if removed.'

My daughter is one year old. I have bought her new swimming costumes to wear on our holiday. Kneeling in front of the washing machine, I can't stop thinking about how my baby daughter is already being subjected to a repression, an othering, that her male peers are not.

When I was shopping, I noticed that these single-use plastic strips were in every swimsuit and bikini, even those for a baby who is just months old. I then searched every rack of boys' swimwear, trunks, Speedos, all ages.

No strip.

Of course not.

The messaging is clear. Girls' bodies are too dirty, too revolting to touch a piece of fabric, from an age well before menstruation could even be imagined. The part of my daughter that one day may bring new life is so disgusting it can only touch this piece of plastic.

I hadn't questioned this before as an adult; it had become part of my conditioning. But as a parent, as I tear out strip after strip of plastic that is as harmful to the environment and living world as it is to my daughter's belief about her own body, I rage.

Our sexual repression and the policing of our bodies starts before our minds even understand why our bodies are being labelled 'unhygienic'. My daughter's perfect, precious body reduced to unsustainable body-shaming slander, at thirteen months old.

UNRAVELLING THE ROBE

Shame has long been a silent force governing women's relationships with their own bodies, particularly in the realms of sex, pleasure and desire. From a young age, we are taught to view our sexuality through a lens of caution, often internalising the idea that our desires are dangerous, our needs are selfish and our pleasure is secondary, or worse, shameful.

This deep-seated shame surrounding female pleasure and sexuality has been pushed on us from the outside as an oppressive narrative that keeps us silent and restrained. Propping it up are societal norms and trends – such as the influence of pornography and the stigmas attached to casual sex and dating.

Sexuality, sensuality and pleasure are all things that we talk about in whispers, if at all. We live in a world where these conversations are either veiled in shame or relegated to the extremes, with little in between. It's either secret, expressed in euphemism, or it's splashed across pages and screens in ways that feel more alienating than illuminating. Where is the honest, open and inclusive conversation that ties together sex, self-care and self-worth?

When we dismantle the harmful myths that have been passed down for generations – myths that tell us that women's desires should be hidden, controlled or subdued – we open the way to reclaiming the right to experience pleasure without guilt, to express needs without fear and to engage in sex without the burden of shame.

We can learn to honour our bodies and our needs, to speak openly about our experiences, and to define our own terms of intimacy and connection, fully embracing our sexual selves. The longing to be touched, worshipped, to be held and to feel safe; to receive, to take our time, to name our needs and allow them to be met.

Shame accompanies these wishes that we dare not whisper to the constant underlying metronome, which ticks away relentlessly with all the things we 'should' have done or do or be before we can receive. So we perform, we 'earn' the scraps that we take quickly so as not to diminish the other. We are reminded not to take too much, for too long, but if you don't flourish you are broken, boring, wrong.

'You are not perfect enough for pleasure,' shame tells us.

This isn't just about sex. It's about rules, those unwritten codes that have governed our lives and how breaking them can be the key to our liberation. And yet, sex cannot be ignored. If we are to live with a true sense of freedom and authenticity that is nothing short of revolutionary, we must embrace our sexuality as part of this.

This is the beginning of the great undoing, the unravelling of the tightly bound robe that has kept us in place for too long. Let it fall away, let it pool around your ankles leaving nothing but yourself. Never allow yourself to forget that this is where your power lies.

The cage is built from the expectations, the judgments and the double standards that have confined women for centuries.

'WE RAGE BECAUSE WE ARE NOT FREE. WE RAGE BECAUSE THE VERY THINGS WE ARE TAUGHT TO BELIEVE WILL SAVE US OBEDIENCE, CONFORMITY, SILENCE ARE THE SAME THINGS THAT BIND US.'

— ANNALIE HOWLING

ASK AND IT IS GIVEN

For years, I was disconnected from my own needs, particularly in the realm of sexuality. I didn't know what I wanted and, even if I had, I wouldn't have known how to ask for it.

There was a time when communication in my relationship didn't feel safe. But it wasn't just about that, it was about me, about this whole land of self that I had never ventured into. It was as if I had lived my entire life on the borders of my own being, never daring to cross the threshold.

Not long before I turned forty, I finally did. I cracked open that door just a bit and I found I couldn't turn back. Opening that door was like opening Pandora's box – the self-discovery that poured out was both chaotic and revelatory. It was terrifying, yes, but also the most honest and healing thing I had ever done.

I am a very sexual, sensual woman. But how many women are like I was, afraid or uncomprehending of their own desires? And how many, when it comes to sex, follow that rule – that lie – that governs so many areas of our lives: 'Don't ask for what you want because wanting is selfish'?

'A LOT OF PEOPLE ARE AFRAID TO SAY WHAT THEY WANT. THAT'S WHY THEY DON'T GET WHAT THEY WANT.'

— MADONNA

A YOGA STUDIO IN LONDON, 2019

'What are your boundaries?' she asked me, carefully following the protocol that our instructor had demonstrated just minutes before.

'None,' I lied, attempting to sound breezy and nonchalant, while simultaneously breathing in, flattening my stomach, wishing to be perceived by this almost perfect stranger as perfect myself.

To be perfect, of course, meant not causing anyone else discomfort. I would be the perfect partner for Sara during this exercise. I would angle my body in the perfect way and give all of the perfect answers and she and the other twenty-five women in this room would believe me to be calm and confident, allowing me to disappear in my internal discomfort.

'Okay, great,' she replied, as she bent down over me, her full breasts with their silver nipple rings glistening in the soft glow of the room. She had talked to me about them and her love of S&M clubs as we undressed together, after being put into pairs. We had stood folding our clothes into neat piles, the same way you would pack away groceries while chatting about your day with your flatmate. Sara seemed so confident, so at home in her body, her experiences, her sexuality.

I was there because I was desperately seeking a solution to save my marriage. I hoped to bridge the brokenness, to fix what would ultimately prove to be unfixable. I thought that it was me who was somehow wrong and destined for a life disconnected to my true sexual nature – whatever that was. I really didn't know.

'Now, decide between each pair who will go first to receive,' encouraged the instructor.

'I can go first,' I said, too quickly. Adding – of course – 'I don't mind.'

Act, perform, brace, smile, Annalie. Don't let anyone see how you feel. Make her think you are so at home with this, with yourself, with your sexuality and pleasure, like you do this every day, my inner critic hurriedly dictated.

The reality was that being the first to receive was also a way of hiding. That is why I went first; this is why I always went first. I was always hiding.

As I lay on my front on my yoga mat, feeling the rubber under my breasts and pussy, my naked body connecting to some warmth and comfort from the mat, I could sink and shrink further into the space that shame had created for me.

Before I closed my eyes, I noticed that Sara looked nervous. This sexual empress, as I had perceived her to be, was gently biting her lower lip in a mix of concentration and something that I couldn't place before making her way to the foot of the mat. The confidence that I had presumed was also acting; she was nervous too, keen to get it 'right'.

'Remember,' reminded the instructor, 'go much slower than you think, allow her to feel every sensation.'

A quick glimpse around the room at all of the other pairs in the soft, low light revealed a palpable sense of discomfort. We had been introduced to each other the evening before and presented with jade yoni eggs at an altar. Now, at 10am the following morning, in a yoga studio in London, we were still strangers but now we were naked, in every sense.

I closed my eyes and I heard Sara exhale. She began sweeping the black ostrich feather that we had been given slowly, so slowly, along my foot.

'Everywhere that there is a crease, remember, that's an erogenous zone,' I heard the instructor say, as the rhythmic pulsations of the erotic music and incense filled the air. 'There is nowhere to go and there is nothing to do, so take your time.'

There is nowhere to go. There is nothing to do, I repeated to myself. This was the permission that I needed to sink into the experience.

As Sara focused on the creases of my body, the backs of my knees and my wrists, my neck, behind my ear, with each slow, languid, intentional and loving stroke of that feather, I felt sensations belonging to the woman that I once was and feelings that belonged to the woman that I had never yet been coming into view. I had been resisting so many parts of myself for so long. I exhaled; my belly became softer; I no longer cared how I looked. Shame couldn't reach me here. The music, her touch, our bodies, the women, the scent, the safety, the sensation, the sensuality, the slow softness.

Everything felt possible from here.

As Sara inched the feather up my inner thigh, she paused. I had said, 'No boundaries.' She then brushed the tip of the fairy-light feather under the crease of my butt cheeks, electricity now building and coursing through my body, the anticipation and desperation for the next touch manifesting like greed, wanting all of it.

The feather started at my neck again, running slowly, so slowly down my back, each vertebra at a time, my mid back, my lower back, following the curve of my spine. Then, with her feathery vane, Sara was stroking my pussy.

I had been reclaimed and ruined at the same moment. If shame could no longer police my pleasure, this opened up an entirely new life for me and one that would cost me my old one.

As the weekend course progressed, each of us became more free, more authentic. Every woman became more beautiful as we got to see more of each other. It was palpable, how each woman cared less and cared more all at once. Caring less about perceived perfection. Caring more about pleasure, our own pleasure.

One of the earliest exercises was sitting in a circle, naked, legs spread, looking directly at and into each other's pussies, then taking a hand mirror and really looking at your own. My pussy had been seen many times before this, of course – waxing, sex, doctors' appointments, having my daughter. But I had never really looked into my pussy until then.

After each of us had looked more deeply into ourselves physically, with curiosity, you began to see each woman blooming into her own true expression, without shame being able to dictate what we 'should' wear, how we should sit, or sound, or smell.

I imagine shame, all of our shame, standing outside the soundproof glass of the studio that day, like a dangerous animal at the zoo. We were unable to hear shame and the racket it usually made.

In one exercise, all of us naked, we flowed through yoga poses, led by one of the goddess-like instructors. This was yoga with an additional twist: we had learned the history of the yoni eggs we had been given and, taking that practice deeply inside each one of us by placing the eggs inside our pussies, and feeling the connections between yoni eggs, pussies, bodies, yoga, movement, women and power, we flowed in gentle union.

Pleasure, pussy, power, purpose. Presence.

Shame was drowned out by pleasure. It was silenced by our collective coven. Shame could not reach any of us there.

We were slowly being helped into our own couture cloaks of desire, interwoven with the most delicate and beautiful pearls of pleasure. And each of us felt like a goddess. At breaks for lunch or to get some air, we had to remind ourselves to put clothes back on. But afterwards, we would rush back to this circle of sensual sorcery that we had created.

The most electrifying sensual experience of that weekend was an exercise that involved undressing your partner for five minutes. This is an incredibly long time to undress someone who has arrived in just jeans and a vest top. So I was grateful when the instructor passed out light cotton kimonos for every pair to use for the exercise, to add a layer, to add time.

'Don't rush,' she said softly, knowingly.

We blindfolded our partner and discussed boundaries again – how many layers they were comfortable with being removed and any body parts they did or did not want to be touched.

One of the challenges that my partner for this exercise had was being able to be with and be in her body. Shame had told her that she could not trust her body, or others. I was so present with her, every part of me wanting her to feel safe, sacred and allowed to be soft. To relax her very understandable defences, even if just for a little while.

I witnessed her connection to her pleasure as I slowly untied her robe and gently slipped the cool, crisp cotton over her bare shoulder, the corner of her mouth turning up slightly, the audible exhale from a place so deeply within her, something she had been holding in and onto for so long releasing, trusting, taking time. I watched her shiver with pleasure, tiny hairs standing on end all over her body, her sensuality appearing like the sun coming out from behind the clouds after so long.

When it was my turn, I relaxed into the safety of our newly established but safe connection. The blindfold again allowed me to close out any shame and turn up the dial of sensation. As my hair, which trailed down my back at the time, was lovingly, delicately and slowly swept across my shoulders, I felt as if I had been plugged in. Sensations of electricity, pleasure and aliveness pulsated through my body from the slightest and lightest touch.

I learned in that moment how sensuality and sexuality were so different and yet it was this point of interconnection that was the North Star of my pleasure. Sexuality and sex can be faked, rushed, performed or masked. Sex can be disconnected in every sense.

Sensuality cannot.

Sensuality is slow, the pleasure from the touch of that feather, five minutes to remove a robe, the sweep of someone's hand across the back of my neck, being assured that you have time and taking it, taking up all of it for your pleasure.

Sensuality is extremely hard because, to explore it, we must be extremely vulnerable.

A CONVERSATION WITH ALEXEY WELSH

Alexey is a holistic intimacy coach. For twenty years he has worked with couples and individuals, helping them to develop their sex life and improve their intimacy and trust.

When I was thinking about shame in the context of sex and sexuality, I wanted to talk to Alexey to find out why people go to him, and at what point of their journey. What does he think stands between women and fulfilling sex? What are the stories that he hears most often? I know that, before I went on the sexual empowerment course, I didn't know how to name my needs at all. How many women out there are in the same place that I was?

We live in a world where sexuality is both hyper-visible and misunderstood. We all carry around certain scripts – deeply ingrained beliefs about what sex should look like, what it should feel like, who we should be within it. But do we question enough how these scripts have evolved – or, perhaps more accurately, how they've been warped?

There are plenty of influencers out there telling us how to have 'good' sex, but rarely do I see them talking about the true intimacy that comes from knowing yourself, from understanding your own needs, from being brave enough to voice them.

And isn't that what we're all trying to do? Whether it's in the bedroom, the boardroom or anywhere in between – we're all trying to find the courage to live by our own rules.

It's not just porn. There are influencers out there preaching about sex in a way that makes it all seem so shallow, so empty. The problem is, they're connecting with an audience who doesn't know any better. People are consuming this information because it's the only source they have. There's no mainstream, reliable sex education out there, no 'BBC of sex', so to speak. And yet, people still trust these influencers more than they trust any kind of official information.

Waves of popular but misguided sexual trends create a new kind of pressure to enjoy something because we think everyone else is, or that is what is expected of us.

ALEXEY: It's like everyone's jumping on these trends, talking about things like squirting as the pinnacle of sexual experience. And suddenly, if you can't do it, you feel like a failure. But the truth is, not everybody is built the same way, and not everyone needs or wants the same things.

I see it with my clients all the time. Women, especially those under thirty, are often just doing what they think they're supposed to do. They're performing without really connecting to their own desires. It's all about pleasing their partners, meeting some standard set by society or porn or some Instagram guru who has no real understanding of intimacy.

In my professional experience, around thirty is when women start asking questions. They start wondering if there's more to sex than just going through the motions. It's like they begin to sense that there's something profound there, something they've been missing. But they don't know what it is, or how to find it.

ANNALIE: Yes, it's like there is a growing awareness that there's more, but you have no map, no guide to lead you there. It can feel as if our entire sexual culture is designed to keep us from ever truly understanding or accessing the depths of what sex could be. We're given tools that are so superficial, they're almost useless when it comes to the real work of intimacy.

ALEXEY: It leaves us in a place where we have to rewrite the scripts. Because the scripts we've been given are so deeply flawed. Women are still struggling with this ingrained idea that their job in sex is to please their partner.

ANNALIE: Even the most successful, confident women – when it comes to sex, they fall into this role of serving the man's pleasure. It's like this unspoken rule that no one ever questions.

ALEXEY: Exactly. It's a new kind of cage, wrapped in the language of liberation. And it's confusing as hell because women are told they're free, that they can do whatever they want. But then they're subtly shamed if their desires don't fit into this new script of what it means to be sexually empowered.

Women start by recognising that they've been fed a lie, and that it's okay to want something different, something deeper. They break the rules, not just for the sake of breaking them, but because the rules were never meant to serve them in the first place.

ANNALIE: It's a journey not just to understand sex, but to reclaim it, to make it something that was truly our own. And in that reclamation, perhaps, we might find the freedom we've been searching for all along.

But in a world where we're constantly being told what we want, how do we ever figure out what we actually need? It's easy to go with the flow, to follow the narrative that's been handed down to us like a sacred scroll. We absorb the scripts without even realising it, until we wake up one day and wonder why our lives, and, more poignantly, our relationships, feel so damn empty.

ALEXEY: Female orgasms are the most oppressive thing at the moment in terms of female sexuality. I believe that the biggest rule that women need to liberate themselves from is the one that states that you need to have an orgasm. That it's impossible to enjoy sex without it. That is an imposed rule.

Women don't tend to ask themselves why they need to orgasm; there's just this directive that they have to do it. To deliver it for their partner, who needs it. And if they don't orgasm, they're not enjoying sex, they're broken. Then they have to work on themselves to solve this 'problem'.

So I think this is the central rule that is limiting sex lives for women. It stops them exploring alternative ways to have sex, to experience connection and desire.

ANNALIE: I think we need to talk about sex, about desire. Not the kind of talk that makes us squirm in our seats or giggle nervously. But the kind that gets to the heart of what it means to be connected – to another, yes, but, most importantly, to ourselves. Because if we don't know what we want, how can we ever hope to ask for it?

I certainly didn't know what I wanted. I knew what I was supposed to want, what was sold to me as the ultimate goal: a connection so profound it would sweep me off my feet, leave me breathless and transform my life. But that wasn't my reality. I aspired to Pinterest-perfect fantasies layered with images that seduced me into believing that good sex was as simple as the Helmut Newton photography that adorned my walls – seductive, dark and slightly out of reach.

It wasn't until I found myself surrounded by a circle of women, all equally uncertain, equally searching, that I began to unravel the truth.

We used ostrich feathers, blindfolds, massages – all things I'd never imagined as part of my sexual repertoire. But it was less about the physical acts and more about the doorways they opened. Doorways to understanding, to desire, to the simple yet radical act of asking: 'What do I want?'

ALEXEY: Here's the thing: you can't ask for what you want if you don't know what's out there. If all you've ever known is a limited experience, how can you expand your horizons?

Most of us stumble through sex like we're walking through a dimly lit room, bumping into furniture and feeling bruised, but unsure of how to turn on the light. It's not that we're not capable of finding the switch, it's that no one has ever told us it's there.

Casual sex is a phrase that gets thrown around like confetti and yet there's nothing casual about it. The chemicals at play, the emotions, the potential for connection or the void left by its absence – it's all too complex to be boxed into something as simple as 'casual'.

We live in a culture that commodifies sex, that reduces it to a transaction. Swipe right, swipe left, trade a few words and boom, you're in. But the truth is, even in the midst of this so-called 'hook-up culture', people are still searching for something more. They may not say it out loud, they may not even know it consciously, but the desire is there, simmering beneath the surface.

Some argue that masturbation is a safer bet. Know your body, keep the bar high, and don't settle for less. I get that. I even agree with it, to an extent. But we're human and humans crave connection.

So what do people mean when they say they want connection? It's the age-old quest, isn't it? The search for meaning, for purpose, for a link to something greater than ourselves.

But what if the connection we're all seeking isn't about finding someone else? What if it's about finding ourselves first?

The problem isn't that casual sex exists. The problem is that we've convinced ourselves that it's all we should expect, all we deserve.

We've commodified not just sex, but ourselves. We've learned to compartmentalise our experiences, to disconnect from the very thing we're supposedly chasing. Social media fuels this. It's the biggest culprit in perpetuating these toxic narratives. It spreads ideas like wildfire, ideas that become the very fabric of our lives simply because they're popular. But just because something is popular doesn't mean it's right. It doesn't mean it's healthy. And it certainly doesn't mean it's what we want.

We need to treat our sexual experiences with the same care with which we treat our nutrition. It's not just about what tastes good or looks good, it's about what nourishes us, what feeds our souls, what keeps us healthy in the long run. Right now, we're gorging on junk food cheap thrills that leave us empty and craving more.

Here's the truth: sex is a powerful force. It's not just about pleasure, though pleasure is a beautiful part of it. It's about connection, yes, but also about love.

Love is the most unexplored and yet the most powerful force in sex.

We've separated the two for so long, as though they belong in different worlds. But they don't. Viktor Frankl wrote that sex is the physical expression of love, and I believe that. We need to start seeing sex as more than just a physical act. It's a spiritual experience, one that requires us to be fully present, fully intentional.

So where do we start? How do we break free from the narratives that have been handed to us and create our own?

The first step is to ask yourself: what do I really want?

Not what you think you should want, not what you've been told to want, but what you actually desire. What kind of experience do you want to have in your life?

Once you start asking these questions, the answers will come. They might surprise you and they might challenge you. But they'll be yours, and that's what matters. And once you know what you want, you can begin to create it.

Sex isn't just something that happens to us. It's something we create, something we shape with our intentions, our desires and our love. It's time to stop asking for permission and start asking for what we really want. Because when we do, we open the door to a life that is not just fulfilling, but truly, deeply alive.

When we bare all to the world shame has nowhere to hide, no further control, for if we allow ourselves to be truly seen, as Emily Ratajkowski so beautifully writes, we can no longer be hurt.

'STRIP YOURSELF NAKED SO IT SEEMS LIKE NO ONE ELSE CAN STRIP YOU DOWN; HIDE NOTHING, SO THAT NO ONE CAN USE YOUR SECRETS TO HURT YOU.'

— EMILY RATAJKOWSKI, *MY BODY*

GOING HOME

On the last morning of the course, at the morning check-in, sitting cross-legged in a circle, I found myself pushing my nails into my palms. The familiar response to pain that I was trying to 'manage' and keep below the surface, in cased it spilled out.

Shame was begging me to perform but I had quite literally laid bare more of myself this weekend with this group than I had in years. I had found parts of myself that I thought I had lost. I found parts of myself that I didn't believe I deserved or could ever be part of my life. I had learned over those days together that shame often has less hold of us in a room full of strangers than when we are with those close to us.

It was my turn to speak. All eyes on me.

'I don't want to go home,' I said, tears pouring, the shame being purged from my body and held in this space.

I didn't want to go home because I knew what that would mean. It meant facing the reality that my marriage was over.

NIKKI'S STORY

Nikki is one of my oldest friends. She is also an acclaimed coach and mentor, and the creator of the female sexual empowerment course through which I found so many parts of myself.

What if you dared to explore your deepest desires? Not the surface-level cravings, but the ones buried so deep that they feel almost too dangerous to acknowledge.

Imagine sitting down with a blank sheet of paper, ready to uncover the truth of what you really want. Not just ten things, but a hundred. A hundred raw, unfiltered desires that cut through the layers of who you think you should be, down to the very core of who you are.

It's terrifying, right? This idea that your desires could be bigger than the life you're living, louder than the relationships you've built, more demanding than the roles you've been assigned.

But what if, instead of suppressing them, you listened? What if you allowed your desires to lead, to shape your life, to become the fire that burns away everything that isn't truly you? Yes, that's terrifying, but it's also liberating.

Because here's the truth: a life without desire isn't even black and white; it is grey. It's a life of going through the motions, of being alive but not truly living.

When I look back on the woman I was, desperately trying to fit into the mould of what a 'good wife' should be, I see someone who was dying inside. I wanted to be perfect for him, to be everything he needed, because I believed that if I could just be enough, I would be loved, and that love would be my security.

But it was all a lie.

I faked orgasms, I faked confidence, I faked my way through life; all the while, my desires were screaming to be heard.

I met an ex-boyfriend during a time when my life was defined by my eating disorder and the all-consuming need to be flawless. I put him on a pedestal so high that I lost sight of myself below. I became the good girl, the one who moaned on cue, who twisted her body into shapes she thought he wanted, who faked orgasms to avoid the terrifying truth of her own imperfection. For years I faked it, convinced that if I just kept up the act, he'd never know the mess underneath.

The message was clear: my pleasure was secondary, something to be sacrificed on the altar of his satisfaction. The shame of this wrapped itself around me like a second skin. I couldn't let go, couldn't let him see that I was anything less than what I believed he wanted. But the cost was high. I lost myself in that performance, burying my real desires so deeply that even I couldn't find them.

When we broke up and eventually came back together, I told him the truth: 'I faked orgasms with you for three years.' His shock was palpable, but saying it out loud was like a key turning in a lock. The door to my real self creaked open, letting in light I hadn't felt in years. It was a revelation, not just to him but to me. The shame I had carried for years was suddenly in the open and it lost its power over me.

What I had never realised was that my body wasn't just a vessel for someone else's pleasure. It was mine to claim, mine to worship.

The journey back to myself wasn't easy, but it began with small acts of rebellion, reclaiming my body, piece by piece. I started to ask, 'What do I want? What does my body crave?' I started to treat myself with the kindness and care that I had always reserved for others. The small rituals, like taking the time to moisturise my body with intention, became acts of self-love. Each touch was a reminder that I was worth the effort, that my body deserved to be cherished. And more than that, I began to believe that my desires were not just valid, but essential.

When I finally began to understand and embrace the beauty of my own body, I realised that my pleasure wasn't a performance, it was a birthright. I began to hold my head higher, to walk with the knowledge that I was the prize. I was the one who deserved to be worshipped.

There's a profound shift that happens when a woman stops seeing herself as less and starts to see herself as something to be worshipped. The power dynamic flips. It's not about being perfect for him anymore; it's about being perfect for yourself. And when I carried that energy, it changed everything. The men in my life began to reflect back what I was putting out. They could only worship me as much as I worshipped myself.

For so long I had been too afraid to even look at my body, let alone love it. But as I stood in front of the mirror, I saw it for what it truly was: a masterpiece. My pussy wasn't something to be hidden or ashamed of. It was powerful, beautiful and deserving of the utmost reverence. This change wasn't just about sex; it was about reclaiming my worth in every aspect of my life. I began to demand more, not just from men, but from myself.

This journey was about much more than pleasure; it was about power. The power that comes from knowing, deep in your bones, that you are enough. That you are more than enough. And when you hold that power, the world shifts. The shame that once held you back dissolves, replaced by a fierce self-love that demands respect, not just from others, but from yourself.

I realised that the shame wasn't mine to hold; it was something that had been given to me by a world that fears a woman in touch with her own desire. Shame is the weapon used to keep us small, to keep us from claiming our full power. We live in a world that tells us to shrink, to hide our desires, to be quiet and compliant. But what happens when we refuse? When we step into our power and claim our pleasure as our own?

We become unstoppable. We become women who know their worth, who demand to be seen and heard, who are unafraid to take up space.

That's why I always go back to: what do you want? We are told to be strong, to move on, to not let it drag on, but this dismissal only deepens the wound. We need to find our voice and keep it, as Madeleine Albright writes.

'IT TOOK ME QUITE A LONG TIME TO DEVELOP A VOICE, AND NOW THAT I HAVE IT, I AM NOT GOING TO BE SILENT.'

—MADELEINE ALBRIGHT

TAKING SPACE

I was struck hard by some profound truths as a result of the workshop in the London yoga studio. The first was that embracing our sexuality means taking up time. And yet, so often, we do not feel deserving of taking up another's time for our pleasure.

'I am taking too long.'

In all senses, we need this time to be with our bodies and also to explore our pleasure, what we want. Most of the women in that room had never been asked what they wanted. What gave them pleasure. Have any of us asked this of ourselves enough? Or does shame and our conditioning get in the way?

'I don't know how to ask for what I want.'

It's as if the race through life, which can be a game of whack-a-mole, ticking off all of the steps, the boxes, the items on the to-do list and hopefully getting the prize at the end, is replicated in sex. We are seeking the wrong prize – that of being 'perfect enough' – to keep us safe for another day of being able to live judgement-free from another.

We've been trained to hide, trained to shrink and contort ourselves to fit into boxes built by others. For so long I believed that to keep love, to keep the illusion of safety in a relationship, I had to be perfect. Perfectly thin, perfectly pleasing and perfectly silent about my own desires.

There is nothing more dangerous to the status quo than a woman who has freed herself from shame. Because when shame no longer has a hold on you, there's nothing anyone can use to control you.

The truth is, the shame we feel around sex, around our bodies, around our desires, is the most powerful tool used against us. It's the leash that keeps us from running free. But what if we let it go? What if we embraced our desires, all of them, and lived from that place of truth? What would happen then?

I'll tell you what happens: you become alive. You become powerful. You become a woman who knows her worth, who knows that her desires are sacred and worthy of being fulfilled. And in that knowing, you become a force of nature.

I used to think desire was something to be ashamed of, something that needed to be hidden and managed. But now I see that desire is life itself. It's the pulse of the universe running through our veins, guiding us toward what we're meant to be. And when we follow it, when we give ourselves permission to want what we want, we are unleashed.

UNHIDDEN

SHAME AT THE HANDS OF THE MEDICAL ESTABLISHMENT

The things all women know. The things we joke about wryly, quietly, for if we don't laugh we would surely cry. The things we go through alone.

Feet in stirrups. Staring up at the strip lights.

'This might feel a little cold!'

The exposure. The discomfort. Awkwardly soundtracked by small talk.

'Shouldn't hurt much!'

It does. It really does.

'Nearly done!'

The wooden tool. The scraping. The deep, awful, scraping.

'All finished! That wasn't so bad, was it?'

Yes. It was invasive and brutal.

But it happens to us all, doesn't it? So we don't make a fuss.

It's for your own good.

Isn't it wonderful what they can do these days?

SCRUTINY

In a world where women's bodies are often objectified, regulated and scrutinised, shame takes root in the most intimate aspects of our lives. At its most dangerous, a sense of disgust turned inwards can stop us from getting medical attention we need. When it comes to fertility and gynaecology, our experiences are frequently marked by a profound loss of agency and a deep sense of betrayal by our own bodies. The shame embedded in the trauma that can arise when we have to undergo medical treatment is not only personal but also deeply cultural, reinforced by a society that marginalises women's pain and prioritises control over care.

When our bodies don't perform according to expectation, or when we are subjected to clinical processes that strip away our dignity, the resulting shame can be overwhelming. This kind of shame is hard to speak of for so many reasons. Sometimes it's simply hard to find the words to express why we feel so violated in a place full of professionals who are trying to help us.

The silent grief of infertility, the trauma of invasive medical procedures, the societal pressure to meet impossible standards of womanhood. Does enduring these things reinforce our inner shameful belief that we are wrong, broken, not good enough?

'WOMEN ARE BORN
WITH PAIN BUILT IN.
IT'S OUR PHYSICAL
DESTINY . . . WE CARRY
IT WITHIN OURSELVES
THROUGHOUT OUR LIVES.'

— PHOEBE WALLER-BRIDGE, *FLEABAG*

COMING OF AGENCY

In the UK, in the months before your twenty-fifth birthday, women receive an invitation. For many of us in possession of a cervix, this is the start of a torturous relationship with the medical establishment in which you will routinely, throughout most of your life, for many reasons connected with having been given the gift of a female reproductive system, be asked to surrender your autonomy and your agency over your body.

The instant nausea, involuntary clenching and deep discomfort from every woman at the mention of the routine procedure of a smear or pap test tells me enough about the collective and unspoken trauma. Of being opened up by a cold metal speculum that winches open your vagina enough so that you can be scraped deep inside your body.

As women, we learn to disconnect and drown out the signals from our bodies from puberty. Repetitive UTIs – oh-so-cutely called 'the honeymoon disease' – then recurrent yeast infections as a result of taking antibiotics for the former. Add in the menstrual cycle, cramps, associated digestive issues, endometriosis or fibroids, which are all 'just part of being a woman'. The excruciating pain of an IUD insertion to manage difficult periods or because contraception is, of course, our job. The list goes on.

So often, we are told, 'It won't hurt.' 'Don't worry!' And: 'No need to be embarrassed!'

But it does, and I am.

If you say that you cannot cope, you are weak. Look around you – everyone else is managing just fine!

Shame.

If this 'doesn't hurt', then no wonder we accept painful sex.

We are told from such a young age and in so many ways to give away our bodies, and we are shamed if we resist. For example, 'Give your uncle a hug!' We are 'cute' when we comply, difficult when we don't.

NAAVA CARMAN

Naava Carman is an experienced fertility, gynaecological and obstetric acupuncturist and herbalist specialising in complex autoimmune disorders such as unexplained infertility. Australian-born, London-raised and educated in the American schooling system, Naava has systematically spent much of her life dismantling the patriarchal structures around the fertility journey and advocating for agency, especially for women of colour. Naava studied Chinese herbs instead of the law course that her parents had wanted for her.

Early in her career, a client came to see Naava heartbroken, having lost a baby conceived through IVF just before the pregnancy was viable. She asked Naava to help her feel better before she began the next round of IVF. Then this client fell pregnant naturally.

This was such an 'aha' moment for me. To experience that a doctor could be wrong, that perhaps medicine didn't know everything.

I wanted to know much more, which I began to learn from both my patients and from medical textbooks. I paid for people's time who were more experienced than I was and taught myself about Western medicine and how to translate it into Chinese medicine. I started to understand more and more about the immune system and the 'wild cards' that affect the things that happen to our bodies for which conventional medicine has no explanation.

I am a firm believer that there's no such thing as unexplained infertility – there is always a reason. When people go to fertility clinics, they often think that they will find out the reason why they are struggling to conceive. However, this is generally a misconception. The clinic is there to make IVF successful, not understand the underlying cause of the issue.

I had a young woman come to me some years ago who had had multiple colposcopies – that is, excisions of the cervix – because she had this 'weird discharge'. We tracked this 'weird discharge' and we realised quickly that she was ovulating and it was in fact cervical mucus.

I see my role and that of colleagues in the field as fertility detectives. We really shouldn't be here; this shouldn't be our job. But we are here to stand between the client and the patriarchy of the old systems, which is embodied in the form of these IVF clinics.

The patriarchy shows up in all kinds of interesting ways when you go down the fertility road. Women are prodded and poked, have blood tests, probes, swabs and tubes inserted, but men are given a semen analysis and that's pretty much it. The number of times that I hear the sperm is in terrible shape but it's still been recommended that a heterosexual couple use an egg donated by a young woman. They never suggest sperm donation, even if there is nothing wrong with the egg. So I guess the feeling among the men who want to go down this route is, 'I don't want a sperm donor but I am fine with my wife going through the gruelling process of IVF and using an egg donor.' It always seems to come down to this underlying, unspoken belief that it is the woman who is responsible. She is often the one who is driving and organising the IVF treatment, and the one who is seen to need to be 'fixed'.

When that hierarchy is deeply embedded in you, it is very hard to challenge. Women are conditioned to defer to men, to authority, to doctors. I step in when my clients need an advocate. I support my clients and I also encourage them to be difficult, to challenge and to ask questions, because being difficult gets you further than being nice and compliant. It makes it more likely that you will be seen as an individual.

The experience of being infertile, whether it is temporary, primary or secondary infertility, is traumatic in and of itself. If you have to use IVF to get pregnant, that may cause you to lose trust in your body to do what it needs to do. By having to involve doctors, you feel that you have outsourced your power. Then, of course, many women will have underlying personal trauma, perhaps from childhood or adolescence. They may have felt dismissed in medical settings or have a partner who is not supportive enough.

I have conversations with my clients – who are often from marginalised groups that are statistically more likely to receive worse treatment from the medical establishment – who unfortunately have been victims of the medical system regarding what their rights are. For example, they have gone in for scans, expressed pain and asked the sonographer to stop, but the sonographer has responded with something like, 'Oh, we just need to see this bit', and kept going. At the point when someone asks the medical professional to stop, they withdraw their consent, so when it continues after that point it becomes what we call digital rape. Obviously further traumatising a woman, who is already in a very vulnerable position.

You cannot separate the mind and the body. They are one thing and must be treated as such. You can do everything that can be done physically, but if trauma is not dealt with then that can be enough to stop things happening in the way that they should. I have known sexual assault survivors for whom sex is very problematic and who are in sexless relationships where the couple is using a turkey baster to try to get pregnant rather than dealing with the trauma. A few years ago, I had a client who disclosed incest. She is still in close contact with her family and the brother who did that to her. In situations like this, with that level of trauma, it seems relevant to ask if the fertility issues are the body stopping another child coming in? Is the body somehow aware that a future child might be exposed to someone who is a threat, who could do that again?

I have to have very difficult conversations as part of my work. You can see how the fertility journey can be long and painful when we have to unravel some of this kind of trauma first.

I don't think women are innately shame-ridden or shameful; I think it is an externally derived emotion that comes from so many sources, exacerbated by how women can be dealt with in medical settings.

UNCHAINED

RELATIONSHIPS
AND BREAK-UPS

Will and Hope were the perfect pair
        Their connection at first was precious and rare
Where Hope was soft, expansive, creative and wise
Will was energetic, directive, a force of nature, but naive at times
Will believed that you could make anything happen, if you only tried
A *force majeure* even greater with Hope by his side
But Hope had grown weary, Will hadn't realised
She had asked him to slow down, to see her with fresh eyes
Hope had changed, she was in bloom, it was her time to shine
Will couldn't stop, he didn't hear her protestations and cries
He was happy when others acknowledged his achievements
He lived to feel their pride
Then one day, Hope lost her voice
Then she lost the light within her eyes

Finally, she lost the magic, the spark was no longer alive

It was too late when Will came home

For Hope had died inside

Will would not rest

He redirected his quest

To bring Hope back to life

But Hope was gone

Will had lost this bond

For without Hope

Will has nowhere to reside

LEAP OF FAITH

In relationships, shame acts as a barrier, inhibiting authenticity, vulnerability, connection and, ultimately, true intimacy. For if we are hiding parts of ourselves away, scared of what we might find, we cannot be truly ourselves with another person. Even though this may be all that we desire. Shame makes us feel unworthy of love and belonging; it makes us fear that if someone were to really know us, they would reject us.

Shame places value on us performing an act in all of our interactions, including sex, one of the hotbeds of female shame. It fuels destructive behaviours, such as people-pleasing, jealousy, control and manipulation, as we attempt to protect ourselves from further rejection or abandonment. Our own shame can intertwine with the buried shame of the other person in the relationship, driving us further apart, isolating us, as we both present what we think we must so as to be 'acceptable'.

How can we know what we really want when we have been told time and time again not to trust our own inner voice? Shame is particularly powerful when it intertwines with the pain of a relationship break-up. Whether the fracture is down to a betrayal, infidelity or simply the end of a connection that once seemed unbreakable, in the aftermath of the end of a relationship, we can be left questioning our worth and decisions. It is all too easy to shoulder the burden of blame, wondering if we weren't enough, if we could have done more or if the fault lies entirely with us.

When a long-term relationship is drawing to an end, there is no map, no clear path, no next steps or guarantees that all will be 'for the best'. The only thing you have is a calling that gets louder no matter how many times you want to drown it out. This is the leap of faith into the uncertain. Yet it may feel hard to hang on to faith if she has been absent for a long time. A relationship breaking down can feel like standing waist-deep in the sea, as wave after wave smashes into you. You might get used to it, might even be able to sustain it, but as time goes on you are so tired. There is no progress, no let-up, no matter how much you keep pushing forwards.

That is why people stay.

That is why when our inner voice, our intuition, calls our soul to another shore, requiring yet another arduous crossing in which we must risk it all, we try instead to silence it. We might drown it out with work, alcohol, exercise, keeping busy, the never-ending to-do list. Anything that means we do not have to stop, even for a second, and face the very real situation that we have been managing to deny and ignore through all of our external activities.

HEARTBREAK

There is something even worse than heartbreak. More painful than saying or hearing the words that confirm it is over.

It is the moment when you wake up and you have dreamed of them. You can still smell them. For a moment, things are still okay, as they were. You are peaceful. You are happy. Then it comes: the searing pain – so sharp, so forceful – arrives and reality, with all of its cruelty, rips away that image.

You are thrust back into the panic of facing another day of forcing yourself through the motions, clinging to fragments of hope that 'what is meant for you will not miss you' – so easy to say and so hard to believe at our lowest times. For there are heartbreaks that come along that are so agonising, so all-encompassing, that you truly believe you will never be okay again.

This is the time of turmoil, when everything that you believed to be true no longer exists and a new reality has yet to form. When you desperately long for 'normal' to return while enduring the punch of grief for the future that you had been building. When you wonder if there is any chance of saving anything at all that you value from the inferno.

This time passes. You will create your new normal. The grief fades. You have already saved the most important thing – you have saved yourself.

STIGMA

Divorce and separation are often accompanied by an overwhelming sense of shame, as a result of the burden society has long placed on those who dare to leave a marriage. In this, as in so many ways, the patriarchy wields shame as a weapon. Generations of women – and their allies – have worked hard to slough off centuries of repression, and yet still here we find a continuing insidious belief that a woman's worth is tied to her ability to maintain a relationship, regardless of her own needs or happiness. This is used strategically against those going through divorce or the end of a long-term relationship, often forcing them to remain in unhealthy situations or to suffer in silence when they do choose to break free. When a marriage ends, it is not just the loss of a partnership that weighs heavily, but also the shame of perceived failure, the stigma of being labelled as 'the one who couldn't make it work'.

In this, we must reclaim the narrative from the clutches of shame and recognise that divorce or separation is not a failure, but an act of courage and self-preservation. By unchaining ourselves from these oppressive forces, we can see divorce not as an end but as a beginning – a bold step toward living authentically and with self-respect.

NARCISSISTS

Sometimes a relationship comes to a natural end. Even when both parties are able to part with mutual respect there can be a fear of going out into the world as a single person – a world that asks us to conform, that expects us to be one half of a couple. When there is no mutual respect, when the other person is trying to impose their own narrative and diminish our sense of self for their own gains, this becomes even more complicated and painful.

I've learned that a narcissist is a master illusionist. They'll make you believe that you've asked for too much, that your mere existence is an imposition on their fragile sense of self. It's a twisted kind of magic, one where you're the ungrateful one, the selfish one, the one who simply can't understand how difficult it is to be them.

They'll have you questioning your empathy, your intentions, even your own sanity. They chip away at your sense of self, like a sculptor with a chisel, until what's left is a hollowed-out version of the person you once were.

I've seen it so many times, in my clients, in my friends, in myself.

We search for evidence that we're not crazy, that we're not the ones at fault. We cling to the scraps, the crumbs of kindness they toss our way, as if those tiny moments of affection are enough to sustain us. But those moments are like flashes of light in a dark room. They're blinding at first, but once your eyes adjust, you see that they only illuminate the emptiness.

The thing about narcissists is that they convince you it's your fault, that if you were just better, more perfect, you'd finally be enough. You'd finally get that attention, that validation, that love you crave so desperately.

But here's the cruel joke: the longer you try to bask in the narcissist's light, the more you see how incredibly ordinary they are. Their light isn't magic – it's a reflection of your own. You're the one who brings them to life, who colours in the blank spaces they leave behind.

Narcissists are like magpies, stealing shiny objects that don't belong to them, always on the move, always afraid of being found out. They live off the energy of others, needing constant validation, constant attention, because without it, they're nothing.

They're empty shells, and they know it.

That's why they run, why they block, why they spin their webs of lies. They fear being seen for who they truly are: ordinary, insecure and deeply, deeply afraid. Once you see through the illusion, once you realise that you're the one with the magic, you can take it back. You can reclaim your power, your sense of self – and when you do, they lose their hold on you.

There is never a grey area when it comes to assault and yet that is what most clients greet me with. Shame, holding them in some way accountable, responsible for the violent violation that they have endured. As Anne Salter writes, we must not take on shame on behalf of the offenders.

> '**WE MUTE THE REALISATION OF MALEVOLENCE – WHICH IS TOO THREATENING TO BEAR – BY TURNING OFFENDERS INTO VICTIMS THEMSELVES AND BY DESCRIBING THEIR BEHAVIOUR AS THE RESULT OF FORCES BEYOND THEIR CONTROL.'**
>
> — ANNA SALTER, *PREDATORS*

SECRETS

'Why did you stay?'

It's a question so often asked, explicitly or by implication, of those who remain in controlling, coercive, abusive relationships. It's a question I have seen clients who have just escaped from those situations ask of themselves.

And yet how can anyone expect us to make rational decisions when we are in a toxic relationship like this? When we are ricocheting around in confusion at a supposed 'loved one' drawing us into their web of fear and shame, asking us to call it home, to pucker up, say please and not to use 'that tone', followed by pleas and promises of peace that we know will never hold. How are we expected to stand back and say, 'Actually, I am going to make a clear and calm decision, from a place of self-compassion?' We can't. We don't.

Shame asks us to keep secrets. To keep up appearances. It tells us that this is all we are worth.

Fear keeps us frozen. Or we fawn. Our bodies trying to keep us safe in a situation riddled with danger.

And at least this fear is familiar. At least the dangers are known. Unlike the risk we feel we are taking if we leave, if we get out. If we feel that we even can. Who knows what awaits us then?

Just as all trauma is trauma, so all abuse is abuse. There are no grey areas here either. I have spoken to women who have been dominated, emotionally abused and constantly criticised by their partner who say things like, 'But he never hit me.'

When you are constantly hurt, belittled, insulted and demeaned by an aggressor who you have allowed into your life, with whom we have been intimate, do you continue to act exactly as you did before?

I didn't. When I found myself in a situation like this, I learned to stop short of saying what I really thought. I learned never to speak the 'unspeakable' into the ether for fear of something happening again. In a sense, it becomes easier the more you shrink, the more you dim your light. When the next wave reaches you, you do not flinch so hard because you have closed part of yourself down; you are numb.

It's not that bad.

They can't control it.

They didn't mean it.

Shame asked me to keep secrets. No one would ever have guessed. I smiled, I performed, I was so fucking perfect. I didn't consider that the secrets shame asked me to hold were not even mine; they were handed to me, making it my responsibility to bury them, to manage them, to run deep into the woods and hide them somewhere that no one could ever find them.

This is why we stay.

BURNED

Months before I had the courage to tell my then-husband that I wanted a divorce, my body was telling me what I needed to hear in no uncertain tones. Still, I did my best to ignore it.

I had become allergic to my exquisite, very expensive diamond and platinum rings. Every time I put them on, angry, painful red sores would appear.

I had the rings cleaned multiple times. My finger was treated with prescription steroid creams. It made no difference. There was nothing wrong with either the rings or my skin. I had no choice but to leave them off.

I suppose you could say that I got to 'try on' the experience of no longer looking like a wife before it happened. Perhaps this was part of the process, giving me the courage to embrace what it meant to be single? I don't know. But it did seem that not only was my body keeping the score, but it was constantly reminding me of it to the point where my rings, the symbol of those marriage promises, were burning my skin.

Much like my burnout years earlier, my body was forcing the issue that my mind was trying to avoid.

THERAPY

My husband was locked inside himself, unwilling to talk to anyone who could help him. But I went. At this point, I hadn't yet understood what was going to be necessary, what I would have to do. My Sunday evening visits to the therapist were a lifeline, a way of temporarily escaping the unbearable volume of what was not being said. So many things had been swept under the rug that I could no longer walk on it.

During one session, the therapist asked me a question. What was something that I could do to 'help my marriage'?

Fuck you, I thought. *I'm the one sitting here, showing up, doing the work, trying. I'm the one standing in the fucking sea here.*

'I know all the things to do,' I said, inhaling and preparing myself to list all of the things that I 'should' be doing to work on the relationship. The sorts of things a magazine would tell you, or Instagram posts. Like I was about to sit some strange exam in extreme people-pleasing and self-abandonment.

But before I could begin my one-woman presentation on what it meant to be a perfect wife, the therapist spoke first: 'How does it feel to be the only one who is prepared to save your marriage, Annalie?'

Oh, God.

For in that one line, that one question, he had given me the answer that my anxious mind had never found, no matter how many books I read or therapy sessions I had been to. I could do all of the things. I could be more perfect, I could please, adapt, preen, challenge, kowtow, suck it up, offer more, ask for less.

But it would always have to be me that did it.

'How does it feel . . . ?' I repeated slowly.

I knew at that moment that the end of my marriage was also for me to start.

I had been manically running around fanning the weak flames of what was left of my relationship so as not to let them go out.

It was time to stand back and let them die.

AMY CHAN

Amy is the author of Breakup Bootcamp *and host of the* Breakup Bootcamp *podcast. She is an expert in dating and has been described by the* Observer *newspaper as 'a relationship expert whose work is like that of a scientific Carrie Bradshaw'.*

Love isn't linear. It's messy and unpredictable. It's not something you can control or plan for, and sometimes it doesn't work out. But that doesn't mean you're broken or unworthy. It just means you're human.

It's about knowing that, even if you fall, you can get back up. It's about embracing the discomfort, the pain, the uncertainty, and believing that you'll survive. Because you will. You don't need to pad your life with guarantees. You just need to trust that whatever happens, you'll be okay.

Women, in particular, are often taught to make themselves smaller, to hide their true desires out of fear that they won't be loved for who they are. But that's not love, that's a performance. True love starts with self-love. It's about owning who you are, standing tall, and saying, 'This is me. Take it or leave it.'

And yes, it's terrifying, because it makes you vulnerable. But it's also the only way to find the kind of love that will fill you up instead of draining you dry.

Some of us convince ourselves that we're better off alone, that it's safer to stay guarded than to risk the vulnerability that love requires. Afraid of rejection, of being hurt or perhaps disillusioned and burned by heartbreak, we resist love altogether. In this place of fear, coming from the belief that everyone is out to screw us over, we might arm ourselves with the latest buzzwords – boundaries, gaslighting, narcissism – and build walls so high that no one can climb them. We collect red flags like trophies, validating our fears with every misstep. And in doing so, we miss out on the possibility of real connection.

I used to be the person who believed in the fairy tale. The one where love is a straight line: meet, date, marry. The kind of love they sell you in Hallmark movies and childhood storybooks. I wanted that so badly, it hurt. Every boyfriend became a potential husband, every date a step closer to the altar.

The fear of missing out on that linear path drove me into a frenzy. I became obsessed with being chosen, as if my worth depended on someone else deciding I was enough. I jumped from one relationship to another, each time projecting all my hopes and dreams onto a person I barely knew. And when it inevitably didn't work out, I crumbled. The grief was unbearable.

But I was chasing a dream that wasn't even mine. It was the dream of my parents, my friends, society. In that space of pain, something beautiful happened. I stopped and asked myself, 'Whose plan is this? Is it mine?' For the first time, I let go of the narrative that had been driving me for so long.

I decided to start living my life for me, not for some future wedding or happily-ever-after that might never come. And in that decision, I found my power. It wasn't something that happened overnight; it was a process, a journey of connecting the dots, of seeing how each past relationship had led me to this moment.

Once I understood that, everything changed. I stopped settling for crumbs. I stopped letting people walk all over me. I learned to recognise the difference between genuine interest and someone just passing the time.

People are clinging to relationships that are long past their expiration dates, afraid to let go because they don't know who they are without that other person. They jump from one relationship to another, hoping to fill the void, but it never works. They end up hurt, confused and even more lost than before.

The truth is, you have to be whole on your own before you can truly love someone else. You have to face your fears, your insecurities, your pain and deal with them head on. Only then can you break free from the patterns that have been holding you back.

And when you do, something amazing happens: the universe shifts, people start to notice, exes resurface, sensing that you've moved on. They try to reel you back in, to reconnect. But you're stronger now. You know your worth and you won't settle for less.

There's a danger in waiting for someone else to save you, to make your life complete. Even if you find that person, it won't magically fix everything. Happiness doesn't come from someone else – it comes from within.

There is no need to chase a dream that isn't yours. The life you want is already within you, waiting to be discovered. It's time to choose yourself.

LUCK

In the early stages of my divorce, I consulted a barrister, a highly sought-after, revered and celebrated man at the top of his game with a 'forensic mind for finances', apparently. What I hadn't anticipated was that this meeting, which I was paying handsomely for, was effectively a masterclass in everything that I could not have. My future life of 'lack' was highlighted quite literally line by line until any hope had been all but extinguished.

This meeting was terrifying. I was triggered, driving my nails into my palms multiple times to stop the tears, languishing in one of the lowest places of lack I could imagine.

But I remembered a key detail, something that the legal system, it seemed, was trying to take from me at that moment.

I was the client.

I had a choice.

And I did not choose this.

Suddenly wild with a kind of internal inferno of indignation and fury caused by yet another man telling me what I could not do, what I could not have, I pushed back. Standing up from the table at the end of the meeting, knowing that I would never employ this man to represent me, I looked him dead in the eyes and said, 'I am the luckiest person that I know and I back myself.'

He chuckled gently.

In that moment, I called back all of my power, all of my luck.

This statement became a mantra to me. It was created in that moment and has served me so many times since. I repeat it whenever I feel myself doubting my relationship with luck and it works every time. Never allow anyone else to determine your luck.

I did not hire that lawyer. I hired a fierce, brilliant woman who had pushed her own luck and that of her clients fearlessly and relentlessly. A bricklayer's daughter who had become one of the first female heads of chambers in the UK, a trailblazer, a badass. She worked as hard as I did and we made our own 'luck'.

So how can you push your own luck?

Luck is very much like a muscle – it is something that we can build and that, critically, we can sustain and enjoy the benefits of time and time again.

Think about it: if you wanted to build a muscle group you would go to the gym and you would train it, repeatedly, over an extended period of time. You would know exactly what you did to get there. Other people may compliment you but it is unlikely that they would call you lucky, as they would be able to see the work that went into this transformation. You would also be unlikely to feel lucky. Happy, positive, more confident and energised, absolutely. But you would know the commitment, consistency and discipline that it took to craft this muscle. You surrendered to the process because you could be certain of the results.

So why don't we feel this way about luck?

How often has something gone well but you cannot be fully present in celebrating and receiving this blessing because you fear that it will be taken away or that this will be 'as good as it gets'? The pressure to receive and revel in the 'only' good times you may have in a while becomes utterly overwhelming.

We are not talking about a winning lottery ticket – these sorts of lucky events are few and far between and act as glorious illuminations that light up anyone's lives. We are speaking of things that you will have strived for, sacrificed for, like the muscle-building example above. You know the steps that you have taken to put yourself in that position.

For we create our own luck. In every conscious decision that we make for ourselves, we are aligning to the role of our soul and we become luckier. So call your power back and remember that Lady Luck is the ultimate cheerleader and never runs out.

'I AM SMART, I AM TALENTED, I TAKE ADVANTAGE OF THE OPPORTUNITIES THAT COME MY WAY AND I WORK REALLY, REALLY HARD. DON'T CALL ME LUCKY. CALL ME A BADASS.'

— SHONDA RHIMES, *YEAR OF YES*

MARK GILMARTIN,
PARTNER, FAMILY LAW

Mark Gilmartin represented me during my divorce process. Mark is a partner at a leading London law firm, often representing individuals of high and ultra-high net worth. He is a fierce advocate for changing the dynamics of divorce and promoting women's rights in the divorce process. Mark is a single father to two young daughters.

At the start of the process, I see a fragility. So often, the woman – a wife, perhaps a mother – seems to shoulder more of the emotional burden of separation. It almost doesn't matter what has happened to bring her to a point of seeking a legal separation, there is anxiety and a fear of change, of what it might mean to leave the dependency unit – or what feels like a dependency unit. In many instances, women have been smothered by this in their relationship, this blanket that suggests you can't do it on your own if you leave.

Would people leave sooner if shame wasn't involved? Yes. Shame and fear go hand in hand. For women, the real shame comes from this sense that they failed at a marriage, at keeping the family together. They feel responsible that their children are going to grow up in a 'broken home'. That old idea still exists. I don't think fathers tend to shoulder that sense of shame as much as the mother can.

But as the divorce process continues – and it is always a difficult process – I see a sense of empowerment and independence begin to emerge. They realise that, actually, they aren't dependent, they are capable and liberated. By the time the case is finished, there is a very marked difference between the woman that I represented at the outset and the woman that they are at the end of the process. This comes about at least in part, I think, through them realising what they want and taking control.

It still shocks me that, in our family justice system, the process enables and facilitates the continuation of a type of abuse that somebody could be forced to endure during a separation. Until just a couple of years ago, perpetrators of abuse could cross-examine their own victims. We've really come forward with changing that in the last few years, but only in the courtroom. In the private arena, when both parties and their representatives sit around the table together, there aren't special measures or protective screens or mechanisms in place that say, hang on a minute, there's a power imbalance here. This is an issue that still hasn't been properly grappled with.

By putting a woman across the table from her husband or the lawyer representing the husband, they can give her that death stare, that look that says, 'I'm going to make you feel ashamed.' There is little to stop someone taking an approach that isn't about fact or the law, but asks: how can we emotionally crush my opponent?

That's not my approach, but it does still happen.

There are therapists out there who could and should be engaged to make this a process of smooth separation that's best for the children, for everyone, not an attack and not a facilitation of continuing abuse. This is what we should be doing now.

Shame is absolutely weaponised in the divorce process. Once, one of my clients told me about the really quite dark fetishes within their intimate relationship. He wanted me to weaponise it. He said to me, 'I know my merits or my prospects are weak, but just a hint at this in the correspondence, just a suggestion of trigger words will bring my ex-partner back to the mindset of that humiliating sexual shame and I believe she will then back down.' It almost sounds like it's bordering on extortion or blackmail. But when there are instructions, within restrictions, limits and ethical boundaries, that's what you do.

I think most lawyers do that. I don't think it is the right tactic or the right approach. We shouldn't be looking at separating couples through the lens of battle and conflict. Divorce doesn't need to become a war of attrition. And it is often shame that is a weapon of attrition – 'Let's pick on someone's vulnerability and make them feel as powerless as possible.'

I remember speaking to a lady whose husband was a very senior, wealthy person working in the financial services. There was clearly something that he had left her with, in terms of fear and shame. We had a first consultation. Then years passed and she stayed with him. Eventually, she came and saw me again. She said, 'I do need to make a move on this. I really, really have to do it. But I need you to tell me that I've got to do it, I need you to force my hand, to make me go through the process, because if I'm given the chance not to, I won't do it, because I'm too scared.'

Of course, I can't do that. And she still hasn't started divorce proceedings, even though they are separated. Now, every year that passes in which she oscillates about whether or not she's going to move on with it is another year of unhappiness, which is really sad.

This is a very wealthy husband and then quite a vulnerable wife. There are two children involved. I'm not a psychiatrist, but from what I know, it sounds very much like she has been living in a narcissistic relationship for a very long time and has this fear and shame of being a failure.

Her children go to private school, they live in a very nice part of the world, in a very lovely home, and in the past, they haven't really wanted for anything materially, but, post-separation, she is made to beg for financial provision. She has been told that this standard of life won't be maintained if she goes for divorce. The husband's assets and resources aren't onshore and so the recovery of those assets in a divorce process would be very difficult for her to achieve. So she knows this is not the life or the marriage that she wants, but she feels like she will be failing her children.

This is a woman who was physically assaulted, who applied for and was granted a non-molestation order, but, in response, her husband withdrew all financial support. He stopped paying the rent, the children's school fees, any allowance. She was completely dependent on this financial support, to the point where she said, 'I have to withdraw the divorce petition. He has told me that the only way I will get another pound is if I move to withdraw it all from the court.' So she put herself back in that situation of risk and fear of violence to survive. To me, it seems astounding that somebody is made to feel that vulnerable.

I have also seen sexual shame used as a tool in divorce in a couple of cases of revenge porn. Photos taken at intimate moments when the women were at their most vulnerable are weaponised. This launches the issue of shame like a harpoon, right into the centre of the case. And it does destroy a person. That the women might not get the house in a divorce settlement is not the battle anymore – it becomes, 'How do I deal with this stain that is left, and this terrible scar?' This is one of the worst types of case.

RESET

There comes a point in our lives when we can't stand up anymore. We are on our knees, sinking into the waves, and we can't go on pretending that everything is okay.

Before I faced up to the end of my marriage, I was trying to do exactly that. I was telling myself that things were sure to get better, we just needed that holiday, for the intense work project to be over. I was backdating a cheque I never got to cash.

I remember how, back then, I threw myself into everything but the truth. I was the queen of distractions, busying myself with work, with social obligations, with anything that would keep me from facing the reality of my life. My marriage *was* failing and deep down I knew it. But I wasn't ready to face it, let alone admit it to anyone else. This was the most anxious that I have ever felt in my life. I would scour internet forums, looking for people telling of how and why they left their partners, explaining that it all worked out okay. I was searching for mothers who had a daughter the same age, women who found love again.

Even better, I would search for people who had a magic formula to fix it all.

I enrolled onto courses, sought help in the form of therapy, discussed my problems with peers, friends, mentors, coaches. I devoured books, online talks, any resource that

I felt might enable me to bring my relationship back to life, that might save it.

What I was really looking for was a guarantee and I never found it.

Of course I never found it.

I was never meant to find it. I was meant to find something much more valuable.

What I found through all of this work was myself.

Every so often, I turned the page in a book and discovered a resonance, a slight *aha*, the briefest encouragement, a glimmer of a truth I could understand. I found moments of reflection and recognition in other people's stories. Just as I hope you have been finding them in these pages.

In my quest to uncover all of the clues that I was hoping would lead me to that pot of gold at the end of the rainbow, a magical marriage-saving fix, what I found instead was my whole unapologetic self.

When I found her, I knew without question that she could never survive inside the container of that relationship. I realised at that moment that it wasn't permission that I needed, or to have someone convince me that everything would be okay. I saw then that it would never be okay if I tried to force this version of myself that I had uncovered into somewhere she had outgrown.

Once I took the only path that was possible, I never felt that anxiety again. The constant fearful thoughts, desperation to find solutions, fake control of situations to try to ensure they didn't happen again – it all left. Gone.

Challenges arrived in their place: lawyers, lockdowns, financial worries, uncertainties. They all took their toll. But nothing could have brought me lower than those months of being isolated within my own experience, silenced by shame, exhausted by anxiety. That had been my loneliest and my lowest.

When I look back on those moments now, I do recall a saying that I found that gave me courage: 'One day your story will be the inspiration in someone else's journey.'

As for my rings – those stones have been reset into a very beautiful necklace that has never once caused an adverse reaction.

'YOU DON'T HAVE TO BE READY, YOU HAVE TO BE COURAGEOUS.'

— ANNALIE HOWLING

EMILY'S STORY

There's a moment in every woman's life when the earth shatters beneath her feet. It's the moment when everything she thought she knew about her world is ripped away, exposing a raw and terrifying new reality. For me, that moment came when my husband looked at me with a blankness that I didn't recognise and said, 'I think we shouldn't be together anymore.'

I wish I could tell you that I saw it coming, that there were signs – whispers in the night, a shift in his gaze, a lingering coldness in his touch. But there weren't. Or maybe there were but I was too caught up in the web of our life together to notice them. I was busy being his wife, his partner, his equal. Or so I thought.

In that moment, as the words left his mouth, it was as if the life we had built together was nothing more than a delicate house of cards, collapsing at the slightest breeze.

I was young when we met, just twenty-two, on the brink of discovering who I was. He was different from anyone I'd ever known – kind, gentle and bright, yet from a world so different from mine. I was from cosmopolitan London, with a life full of diverse experiences, while he hailed from a small village in the north, steeped in farming traditions. The contrast intrigued me, made me feel like I'd found something rare, someone who could offer stability and security in a world that often felt uncertain. We grew serious quickly and it felt right. We both wanted the same things: a future together, marriage, a family. I felt safe with him in a way I had never felt before.

But as our relationship deepened, something darker began to surface. His bouts of sadness, which at first I thought were just part of his nature, soon revealed themselves as something more. He was struggling with depression and neither of us was equipped to handle it.

His depression was overwhelming, manifesting in intense bouts of tears and emotional breakdowns that left me feeling helpless. I was always the optimist, the glass-half-full person, while he was drowning in a sea of negativity. I became his crutch, the one person he could lean on, and I took on that role with a sense of duty.

I had seen my mother navigate life after my father's death, raising two children and managing her own grief. I thought I could do the same for him, be the rock he needed. But as time went on, our relationship became less about us and more about managing his illness.

I was there through the doctor's appointments, the therapy sessions, the medications he was so afraid to take. I supported him, carried the weight of his depression on my shoulders, all the while trying to hold our relationship together. It was exhausting but I didn't see another option. This was what love was, wasn't it? Being there through the hard times, no matter what.

Then, the tables turned. I developed an eating disorder, anorexia, that consumed me just as his depression had consumed him.

Our relationship shifted again, with him now trying to support me through my struggles. But I didn't need him in the same way he had needed me. I had a strong network of friends, a resilient mother and a fierce independence that meant I often faced my demons alone.

Yet, I could see how the balance in our relationship had tipped, how the person I once was had been eroded by years of caring for him, and now, by my own illness. Looking back, I realise that the foundation of our relationship was built on a fragile sense of security: his need for support and my low self-esteem. I was drawn to his kindness, his niceness, but, if I'm honest, he wasn't really my type. I stayed because it felt safe, because I thought that's what love was supposed to be.

Shortly after our wedding, after a beautiful ceremony that had been postponed multiple times, and a seemingly perfect holiday in Mexico, he dropped a bombshell. We had just been on this incredible trip and I thought we were happy.

He told me that things were shifting between us. He didn't know if this was what he wanted anymore. I was blindsided. How could everything change so suddenly? One moment we were planning a future together, and the next he was telling me he wasn't sure if he wanted any of it.

It was like the ground had been ripped out from under me and I was left freefalling, grasping for something solid to hold on to. The shock of it all was almost too much to bear.

In hindsight, I can see the cracks that were always there, the signs that maybe we weren't as solid as I had believed. But at the time, it felt like my whole world was collapsing, and I had no idea how to put the pieces back together.

It wasn't just the shock of losing my husband that broke me, it was the realisation that I had been living in an illusion. I had convinced myself that our marriage was strong, that we were invincible. We had exchanged vows that we both believed in – or, at least, I did. We had been planning to have a baby. We had just celebrated our anniversary, surrounded by friends and family. He had cried during our wedding, for God's sake! How could someone who seemed so full of love, so committed, turn into a stranger overnight?

But the truth is, he didn't turn into a stranger overnight. I just hadn't seen him clearly before.

When I asked him if there was someone else, he hesitated. There was: a woman at work he had been spending more time with than I realised. But instead of coming to me, instead of talking it out like we had with every other challenge we'd faced, he had built up this narrative in his head. This must mean we shouldn't be together, he thought. And just like that, he pulled the rug out from under our life.

I didn't want to believe it. I gave him a few days to come to his senses, to recognise that he was being dramatic. We could talk about it, go to therapy, do whatever it took.

But he didn't come back to me. Instead, he became someone I didn't recognise, someone cold and detached, someone who no longer saw me as his partner but as an obstacle in the way of his new life.

I had to face the fact that the person I had trusted most in the world had betrayed me in the worst way.

He had shattered my life, our life, without a plan, without any idea of what would come next. But the worst part wasn't even his betrayal. It was that I had given away so much of myself in this marriage.

I had given him access to everything: my heart, my home, my finances. When the lawyer's letter arrived, it was like a punch to the gut. I had no idea that by marrying him, I had given him access to all of my money, my pension, my savings. It was as if I had been blindfolded, led into a contract that I didn't fully understand, and now I was paying the price.

I felt betrayed not just by him but by myself. How had I allowed this to happen? How had I, a strong, independent woman, become so dependent on someone else? How had I handed over my power so willingly?

In the darkest moments, I doubted myself. I doubted my ability to survive this, to rebuild my life from the ashes. But then something shifted. In the end, I saw that this was about more than money, more than betrayal. I had been through hell before. I had fought my way out of an eating disorder that nearly killed me and I had survived. This was just another battle, another test of my strength. I remembered who I was, who I had always been: a fighter, a survivor.

I started to see things more clearly. I started to see him clearly. I had always given him too much credit, believed that he was stronger, better, more capable than he really was. But, in reality, he had been leaning on me, relying on my strength, my resilience to carry him through. And when I no longer served that purpose, he discarded me like I was nothing.

But I am not nothing.

I am everything. I am strong. I am resilient. I am powerful. And most importantly, I am free. As I began to reclaim my life, I learned it was about rediscovering who I was outside of this marriage, outside of him. It was about reclaiming my power, my identity, my future.

I started to write again, to pour my pain, my anger, my grief into words. And, in doing so, I found my voice again. I found my strength. I found myself.

And so, in the end, I am grateful. Not to him, not to the man who broke my heart and shattered my world, but to myself. I am grateful for the strength I didn't know I had, for the resilience that carried me through, for the power I found within. This is my story. It's not a story of a broken woman, but of a woman who refused to be broken. A woman who, in the face of betrayal and loss, found herself again. And, this time, she won't ever let herself go.

LEONIE'S STORY

We'd been out separately that night, both with friends, but we stayed connected, messaging back and forth. When I got home I saw six missed calls, and I felt amazing, like I was the centre of his world.

But the next day, when I sent him a message, something was off. It didn't go through.

I thought maybe he was travelling. He had mentioned a trip to go and visit his family. One tick only – he must be on the plane. But as the hours passed, that gnawing feeling in my stomach grew.

I found myself googling his home country to see if there had been a storm or power outage. I grasped at anything that could have caused the message not to have been delivered.

It wasn't until I went out for a run, a day later, trying to clear my head, that the truth hit me. What if I'd been blocked?

When I got home, I sat on my bed and opened Instagram. And there it was. Or rather, there he wasn't. He was gone. Vanished. Deleted me from his life as if I never existed. In that moment, the floor disappeared from beneath me. I was blocked on Instagram, erased from his life like a mistake he couldn't bear to think about.

I stared at that photo, at his face, and wondered if I ever really knew him at all. I felt worthless, replaceable, and utterly alone.

I thought back to the beginning – how we'd laughed together, how the sex was electrifying, how he'd promised me that once he had the capacity, once work was less crazy, he'd commit.

I believed him. I'd wanted to believe him.

I'd been burned before by men who lied, who cheated, who had addictions. But this had felt different, healthier, more honest. But it was just another lie, another illusion.

A week later, Facebook suggested a new friend, a woman I didn't know. But there he was, in her photo, smiling with her and a puppy. He'd said he didn't have time for a relationship, but clearly that wasn't true. He just didn't have time for a relationship with me.

He erased me because facing me, facing the truth, was too much for him to bear.

And there it was, the realisation that everything I'd thought we had, and that we could have in our future, was a lie.

What I didn't see then, but I see so clearly now, is that I was never the one who was lacking. He was.

When he blocked me, he wasn't just running away from me – he was running away from himself.

UNBOWED

WHEN FRIENDSHIPS NO LONGER SERVE US

We learn early not to meet the eyes of men who may lust after us. But so too do we understand that we must not attract the attention of women who may judge us. Who could shame us for standing out.

'You think a lot of yourself.'

'Who does she think she is?'

How can we claim to polish each other's crowns if we are the first to tear each other down?

So we hide in plain sight. Always careful not to draw attention to ourselves. Keeping quiet. Modest. Demure. And we are rewarded for this, for this is exactly what we are supposed to do.

It's like the game we played as children. Stay hidden as long as possible. You do not win if you are seen.

Don't stand out. Keep completely still. Be silent.

Don't get caught.

Hide.

Win.

THE CUCKOO COMPLEX

The cuckoo in all her cunning lays her eggs in another bird's nest. She never builds her own, never works to craft something herself. She takes. She usurps. She thrives on the efforts of others, leaving destruction in her wake. The cuckoo will always come back, looking for more, but she will never find what she's truly searching for.

The cuckoo complex is the ticking time bomb of relationships built on envy, insecurity and entitlement. When a woman envies you, even slightly, she is not waiting for you to shine; she is waiting for you to decline. She wears masks, she imitates, but any admiration she displays is poisoned by the bitter taste of her own inadequacy. She doesn't believe she has the skills, the strength or the staying power to create her own success, so she takes yours.

This hurts you and it hurts her. Living like this – stealing, pretending, fearing – is exhausting. No one can maintain an act indefinitely without damage, without something cracking. It comes back to that same fundamental truth: you can't fill an internal void with external things. You can't satisfy a deep, aching need with surface-level distractions.

The cuckoo needs to learn to build something of her own. One day, she will have to face up to this. We need to recognise this complex for what it is: a pattern of taking; taking without ever giving back.

NO LONGER A
SAFE HARBOUR

It is always hard to leave a romantic relationship that no longer serves us, or to heal that broken heart from someone who has left us. When things like this happen, it is our friends to whom we go for love, support and compassion. And we in turn give them those things when they need us.

But what about when it is a friend who has broken your heart and trust?

When they are no longer a safe harbour?

When friendships become cold, distant or disconnected?

Maybe you bonded over shared experiences, a break-up, a job, a common struggle. But as time passes, you realise that what once connected you now feels flimsy, like a bridge swaying in the wind.

There's often a moment when you realise that a friendship that you had felt was so strong, so secure, has been untethering for some time. Jokes are no longer enjoyed, invitations stop, they have less and less time for you, though they appear to for others. You find yourself replaying every conversation to see when the fracture began – *Is it something that I've done?*

There is no subject area that I get asked about more often than declines and difficulties in friendships and no question that resonates more deeply and painfully. Every woman I know, myself included, has at least one story of heartbreak or betrayal at the hands of a friend.

What I know to be true is that my greatest friendships involve those closest to me being able to call me out on my shit – kindly. And I would also do the same for them. There is such power and value in this. When we show up authentically for each other, with integrity, friendship bonds remain strong and are one of the most precious things we can have. For shame cannot exist in these kinds of friendships. There are good souls out there, and if I had tried to cling to some of the 'friends' who let me down, I would have missed out on the beauty of life and how the right people really can and do find you at the perfect time.

As women, we are often so entrenched in the deep cycle of people-pleasing that we have learned to avoid conflict at all costs. Being a 'good girl' means not raising our voices, not calling things out or 'making a fuss'. We monitor, assess and analyse people's motivations and responses to us. My work with clients and my own experiences has led me to jokingly refer to passive aggression as 'the universal female superpower'. Of course, men use this tactic as well, but it is not safe for women to be noticeably 'aggressive' even when slighted. So our hurt and discomfort leaks out indirectly, unacknowledged. Or else we turn it back on ourselves, wondering if we are somehow at fault. 'It must be something to do with you,' insists the inner critic. 'You're not very likable, so what do you expect?' shame sneers. This shame can be particularly potent because it attacks us in the most vulnerable spaces of our lives – the places where we expect to find support, love and safety.

When my marriage was failing, one day I finally found the courage to tell one of my then closest friends the truth when she asked me how I was: 'unhappy, scared, breaking'. She cried, so visibly hurt that she hadn't known about my suffering. She pledged her support for me and my daughter. She assured me that I would not need to be afraid for I had her friendship.

And for a short time, I did. When my divorce rattled on over periods of lockdowns and isolation, she faded into the background.

Still, I was there for each of her break-ups, to unpick every detail of a message, to remind her of her power when she felt she had none. I had extended invitations and made my home her own on many occasions.

I knew when she was okay again as I wouldn't hear from her for great swathes of time. And I knew when she was struggling as, almost out of the blue, a message would come in. 'How are you?' it would start. Which we both knew was not an enquiry about my welfare but a prelude to a request. Still, I responded as I knew she wanted me to. Time and time again.

Until I didn't. Until I couldn't take the hours away from the fine balance of plate-spinning that single parenting brought me. Then I placed a boundary that I would support her but I would not on this occasion be able to try to fix this for her as I had leapt in to do so many times before.

The calls stopped coming.

I had been given a piece of advice that was one of the most valuable lessons I could have received at that time: people whom you thought would always be there for you won't necessarily be. Don't panic. As painful as this will be, there will be people who will step in, step up and surprise you in a way you never imagined that they would.

A long-term friend let me down. That would have been heartbreaking had it not been for those – some of whom were little more than strangers at the time – who offered their hands, hearts and homes to me and my daughter in a way that I could never have foreseen and will never forget.

I now know that it is necessary to create distance when I believe a situation or individual to be dangerous in some way. My friendships are now more diverse and I have much stronger boundaries. I also show up differently in my close friendships – always as my full self. I ask for help when I need it and I give my love and support to those who deserve it.

FRENEMIES

A betrayal at the hands of a friend is a unique kind of loss that carries its own brand of shame. Friendship break-ups can be as brutal and as painful, if not more so, than romantic break-ups.

We share posts on social media, celebrating each other's successes, but who is the first to disappear when we falter, or worse, when we start to soar? Who is notable by her absence when we need support the most?

It is bad enough to be let down by someone whom we believed would show up for us when we needed it, because that is what we have always done for them. But what about when those we trust with our deepest fears and insecurities turn on us in the most unexpected way? This is the truth of frenemies, the ones who smile to your face and whisper behind your back. It's as if they become snatchers in the night, taking our secrets, our vulnerabilities, and dangling them over us, threatening to shatter whatever fragile sense of self we've managed to construct.

Some so-called friends have taught me more about covert narcissism than any textbook ever could. They were mirrors reflecting back the parts of me I was too afraid to see. I could have walked away, chalked it up to bad luck, but instead I chose to stay and learn. The universe had placed them in my path for a reason, and I was determined to find out why I had put their needs so far above my own.

It's easy to say that we're all in this together, but the reality is far more complex, far more painful. In a world that mistrusts and diminishes us, we turn to others for safety. But there may come times when people who have been by our side, the ones who've shared our history, whom we were assured would 'have our backs', are revealed to have been polishing a knife to stick in it instead.

Friendship is often a source of deep connection and joy, but it can also be a breeding ground for one of the most painful forms of shame – the kind that arises when those we consider close friends won't cheer for us. When frenemies subtly undermine our achievements, or when covert narcissists manipulate us for their own gain, the sting of shame can be overwhelming.

You cannot be friends with someone who envies you.

You cannot trust someone who is waiting not for your rise but for your fall.

They may take what isn't theirs, but they can never keep it. Because the truth, like a cuckoo's call, always comes in the end.

And when it does, you'll be ready to spread your wings and fly, leaving them behind in the old empty nest that you have outgrown, the nest they tried to steal.

Every time we people-please in an attempt at connection,

we are rejecting the essence of ourselves. What is the cost of losing our true self in exchange for 'fitting in' as so perfectly described by Brené Brown?

'THE OPPOSITE OF FITTING IN IS BELONGING.'

— BRENÉ BROWN

DISMANTLING THE CAGE

At its best, the world of women is a powerful, liberated, supportive space. But it doesn't help anyone if we fail to acknowledge the times when it is a battlefield, a cruel and twisted version of *The Hunger Games* where the real enemy isn't the oppressive system, but the women forced to fight within it. Then, we are pitted against each other, taught to compete in the most vicious of ways. They sometimes call it 'girl code', but it's a code designed to keep us divided.

If you know the real effects of shame, you will never knowingly wish it on another.

We must remember that the fight is not with each other. It is with the systems that have told us we must compete, that we must tear each other down to rise. These systems goad us to turn on one another and then mock us for infighting, for being 'bitchy'. 'Where's that sisterhood now?' they ask sarcastically. When we judge other women for being too much or too little, bossy, outspoken, frigid or slutty, we are internalising the system that keeps us down and we turn our pain and our shame on each other. We claim to wish to fix each other's crowns, and yet when we see a woman begin to rise, it is one of her kind, led by shame, who is the first to tear her down.

But the cage they try to keep us trapped within is not just external – it's also internal, built from the lies we've been told and the lies we tell ourselves. We have to take responsibility for our part. Because the cage can be dismantled, bar

175

by bar, if we learn to love ourselves unapologetically and support one another without judgement.

Shame imposed by others' insecurities is not ours to bear. True integrity comes from standing in our power, from honouring our own needs and desires, from living authentically and unapologetically. It's something you cultivate from within. It's about making choices that honour your truth, even when it's hard, even when it means disappointing others. It's about living in a way that allows you to rest your head on the softest pillow of all – a clear conscience.

When we can do this, we will be filled with the courage to shine brightly, even when others cannot or will not cheer us on.

We can honour our own worth and that of others. We can build solidarity with those on the same journey as us and we can travel together. We can't do it all alone. To isolate ourselves from others because we are afraid of being vulnerable, of exposing the parts of us we think will be rejected, only keeps us isolated and feeds shame.

It is up to us to see all toxic relationships for what they are and to reclaim our power by stepping out of the shadows they cast. Then we can choose our travelling companions wisely and wholeheartedly cheer each other on.

'MAY THE SHAME THAT WE ARE TRAINED TO PUSH DOWN DEEP INTO OUR SYSTEMS OPEN A NEW WAY TO LOVE.'

— ANNALIE HOWLING

IRINA'S STORY

Irina first came to the US on a work travel programme. She started working in a New Jersey motel cleaning the toilets, a job that not even the housekeepers at the motel wanted due to the rats. She is now a leading figure in the world of PR. She is beautiful, magnetic and evidently very successful. Now, she is met with envy from other women. But growing up poor and putting herself through university in Russia, she suffered bullying and shaming from her female peers.

I grew up in a small town in Russia. My family, they're not rich; still to this day I've never received a Christmas gift. My mom would get chocolates, things like that, given to her from different people. She would put them together and that was my present. She would buy something for herself but that would be my gift.

My aunt lived in Moscow. When I was a teenager, I asked my family if, for my birthday, they could buy me a train ticket to go to Moscow and they did. While I was in Moscow, I applied to universities. I was accepted by several, including by the main University of Economics in Russia. When I told my parents they said okay, you can go there, but we don't have money to support you.

My classmates there were from very rich families. For New Year's, one of my classmates was once given a three-bedroom apartment in the centre of Moscow.

I lived in a one-bedroom rented apartment. A random guy was living there in one room and I shared the tiny bedroom with another girl. We didn't even have money to buy two different beds, so we had to share the bed that came with the apartment for five years. I lived on pasta with ketchup and some canned tuna. That's all I could afford.

But I was determined to make the most of the opportunity I had. I was always smart, I was always curious, I had good grades. So my classmates were my friends and the professors always liked me.

Once, some of my classmates, a group of girls, invited me to a nice restaurant. I knew I couldn't afford it. That restaurant was on top of a shopping centre and they wanted to have a walk around it first and buy some things. I pretended that I was looking for something. I wasn't, of course. I knew I couldn't buy anything.

They knew that too.

When it was time to get lunch, I realised I didn't know where they had gone. So I called them but nobody picked up. So I just started wandering around, to see if maybe I could find them. They were already sitting at the restaurant table ordering food.

Naively, I thought I could join them and not eat anything. I said, 'I was looking for you!' and was about to sit down.

Then one of the girls – who I had thought was my friend – said, 'Irina, you're not welcome, because look at us, and look at you. You cannot afford anything here.'

I was very upset, but I knew it was true that I couldn't afford it.

It took me years to realise that that trauma of that moment lived with me for all those years.

At that moment, I promised myself that I would do anything so as never to be in that position again. And while I was trying to achieve those things, I would never treat people like they treated me.

When I graduated, I got a good job. Those first few months of earning money felt amazing. It was intoxicating to buy nice things with my own money. But after a while, I realised I didn't feel anything anymore. I wasn't experiencing that fulfilment or joy. You think the more you get, the more fulfilled you will feel, which is not true.

This is when it got dark because I was lost. At that time, I didn't have any tools. I didn't know much about spirituality and meditation; I had no idea what was wrong with me. I had no idea what to do. And because of that, I felt that the only way was to just keep doing what I was doing.

Now I'm convinced that, if something doesn't work for you, you have the power to rewrite your story. Everything in life is about narrative. I learned this when I began working in PR. Sometimes you change the story for a client, so I thought, well, if it goes this way in a professional environment, why don't we take control of our personal lives and change the narrative we tell ourselves?

Perfection does not exist, because our idea and perception of it is constantly changing. When something is too rehearsed, too obviously crafted, you cannot relate to that image or to that person. Really successful people don't have everything scripted because it's fake. It's the same with life.

I think it's so easy when you look at my life right now to think that, because I have this degree from Wharton, and a very good job, and I know interesting people, I have had it easy. But when I look back at my life ten years ago, fifteen years ago, twenty years ago, I'm a completely different person. I had to go through very uncomfortable experiences and I had to create the life that I have right now, which was never easy.

UNAPOLOGETIC

A LIFE WITHOUT SHAME

One day you have had enough. You will not carry this bag around with you anymore. You have an idea. What if there is something in the bottom of that big bag of Shame that can actually help you? So you start trying to unpack it, but it is heavy, spiky and unruly. You need help, so you call a friend.

You tell them about Shame, expecting rejection or shock, but they smile. They carried Shame too. They know how to help.

The contents of the bag are still too much. You need additional pairs of hands. So you call for more backup from people that you love. It turns out that they have all dealt with Shame and they too know what to do. Seeing this, you feel closer to them than you have felt in a long time, maybe ever before. They come to help you.

You notice that everyone not only took off their shoes when they arrived but they also left the masks they wore to pretend they were always fine by the door.

Shame is much smaller now. Its roots are gone. You can hold it in your hands. It seems weaker and sad.

You reach the bottom of the bag and there it is, the cure for Shame: self-compassion.

You use the memory of a time when you honoured your own needs, mix in the love from the friends who came to help and, lastly, add a drop of courage you gained from what you have just gone through.

And, just like that, Shame is gone.

MORE THAN ENOUGH

'Just the two of you for dinner?'

'Yes.'

I don't believe that anyone at the beautiful resort my daughter and I had travelled to who asked me that question wanted to shame me. But it was asked again and again on that holiday, and it was not what I wanted to hear. Despite me knowing that leaving my marriage was the right path, there were days that weighed heavily in the unravelling.

To ease my discomfort, or if the tears felt too close that day, I would sometimes respond light-heartedly, 'Yes, she is more than enough!'

Which I always meant, but not in the way the maître d' or server or nosy fellow holidaymaker probably heard it.

It is never any hardship to spend time with my daughter. Amber is a blessing, a truly golden soul wrapped in human form. Spending time with her is like basking in the golden hours of the sun. She is and always will be more than enough.

We were on our first solo holiday together, a last-minute decision. We had flown twelve hours to a tropical paradise where the juxtaposition of the beauty and serenity of our location and the chaos of my life crashed together like the waves on the beach.

I was determined to give this little girl, my girl, a great trip.

I was the only adult there not in a couple or with family or friends. I hadn't anticipated the looks of sympathy I would receive, or how agonising I would find them at that time.

'Poor girl,' I heard one couple say.

I looked around to see who they were talking about and realised that they meant me.

I bristled. I was not a 'poor girl' on that trip. Or on any other with my beautiful child. Being her mother is the greatest privilege of my life. Amber gave me family.

Amber was not a poor girl either. Aged three and half, she wore her blue Cinderella dress on the beach and danced to the DJ. We had a party in our room and jumped on the bed (something she was not allowed to do at home) to her favourite Taylor Swift songs. Amber can still remember the time we got caught in a tropical storm. I had to balance an umbrella and wade through water, carrying her on my back. We were laughing so hard we drowned out the geckos' calls on our beach villa's walls.

One night at a dinner, while we were watching the giant fruit bats doing their nightly swooping around, playing a game of tag at another magical sunset, a couple with a child Amber's age sat close by. The atmosphere on that table was overflowing with their resentment towards one another, their criticism of each other's parenting. They took turns to eat while the other looked at their phone.

And yet still they gave me those familiar looks of pity. *Just the two of you?*

At that point, something clicked and my shoulders dropped from their position up around my ears. The glances, the judgement and the pity didn't matter. None of it had anything to do with me and my daughter. I had felt so much peace since being there. I had done the right thing. I knew that. I was taking the first, fledgling steps of my new life and they were happy ones.

At that moment, the restaurant's lights went out, and sparklers and a cake arrived at the table of the couple at the next table, waiters, staff and guests singing and cheering.

'Happy Honeymoon' the glossy chocolate sauce read on the special dessert plate.

Everyone in the restaurant raised their glasses and I in turn raised mine, along with a smile.

All is never as it seems.

In my darkest moments it wasn't the light I was seeking, it was hope. These words by Michelle Obama inspired me.

'DON'T EVER UNDERESTIMATE THE IMPORTANCE YOU CAN HAVE BECAUSE HISTORY HAS SHOWN US THAT COURAGE CAN BE CONTAGIOUS AND HOPE CAN TAKE ON A LIFE OF ITS OWN.'

— MICHELLE OBAMA

DESIRE

Finding your purpose in this life is often talked about in terms of finding something that 'makes you feel alive', but if your life is devoid of desire, it is like trying to start a fire in the rain. You may get sparks, possibly even a tiny ember, but it cannot sustain itself within the conditions around it, which remove its warmth, its light, its hope.

If you have ever watched me in an interview or video, somewhere on my body in the form of a decoration or adornment there will be a snake. In Sanskrit, *kundalini shakti* means 'serpent power'. In some spiritual practices, this divine feminine power is believed to lie coiled at the base of our spine, a powerful, energetic flow that, when activated, connects us to our sensuality and divine love. The snake is also a symbol of infinity, most often with the snake forming a circle, its tail in its own mouth, no end and no beginning.

The other thing that I learned about the snake is that it must shed its skin or it will die. As the snake grows, the capillaries between its scales spread apart, ready for its next transformation. Bigger and bolder than before, it can no longer physically fit inside its old skin and so it is ready to be rebirthed.

So it sheds what no longer fits, what has come to constrain and restrain it, causing it some pain. Eventually, the skin that has been home to that snake slips away, with the snake neither resisting nor clinging on to what was, simply trusting and releasing. This is why, if you are ever to find a snake's skin that it has discarded, it will be inside out.

The snake's metamorphosis is one that sets it free time and again.

The snake has visited me in dreams in the depths of my divorce and given me warnings. The snake has visited me more than once in my real interactions, albeit disguised, at least at first.

I was the snake.

I was dying.

I was going to continue to constrict myself, my potential, my life, the longer I tried to stay within this skin that I had so evidently outgrown.

The reason I wear the snake as an emblem is to remind me of the moment I rediscovered my pleasure and the energy of desire, bringing its mischievous, delicious aliveness into my daily routine. Once discovered, or rediscovered, it can be like a heady fragrance that you excitedly spritz on yourself, your body, your centre of pleasure – the feminine in its most divine expression.

I had been denying myself, hiding away parts of myself for so long. Putting pieces of me into little velvet drawers like those in an old-fashioned jewellery box, waiting for an occasion to wear them again. This was death by a thousand cuts, I thought, a life without pleasure. It was a huge relief to me that I was not broken, that I could be 'rewilded' into life, into my own true, unapologetic nature, in its fullest expression.

There you are, I thought. By you, I of course meant me. The real me, the entire me, the sacred, sexual, scared, scarred seductress. She was all of me.

It's desire that is the bedfellow of aliveness; the times that I have felt the most alive, I have been in the magnetic flow of desire. The dream job, the dream man, the dream life that I wanted for myself. As soon as any of these things come into view, it is desire that has become the fuel.

My own field of dreams grown from the seeds that I have planted.

Desire and pleasure, like a pair of enchantresses, taking me by the hand and leading me into my own Garden of Eden.

CLOSURE

Closure is something that we can become so desperate for. When relationships end, friendships break down or family members have caused us pain, we can entertain a fantasy in which we imagine an audience with the individual in which all loose ends are tied up, questions answered and lack of understanding resolved. We imagine that we will then be able to continue our life with a renewed sense of peace and confidence, all ghosts laid to rest.

In my experience, and in that of many of my clients, that is usually far from the reality. For when we think about this more carefully, we can see that someone who has betrayed and deceived us is very unlikely to give us any sort of meaningful truth. If they could not offer you compassion before, if their actions made you feel shame, it is unlikely that they would offer you comfort now. So the question then becomes – why would you put that sort of power in the hands of someone who has already shown you their lack of integrity?

When we understand this, we can see that the only solution is to find closure for ourselves. For this, we need to place the trust back within ourselves, reclaiming our power, rather than relying on any other person to validate us or to chart our course for the future.

Perhaps some more conversations will be had in the future. Perhaps they won't. It doesn't really matter. Because real closure comes when you realise that you will be okay no matter what, no matter what happens to you, no matter how somebody else acts, no matter the life events that may unfold. True power comes from knowing you will be able to weather any storm.

Always be suspicious when you are encouraged to seek something vital outside of yourself. Closure can only come from within.

ASHLEIGH'S STORY

Ashleigh Warren featured in the US reality TV dating series Swiping America. *She is an author, entrepreneur and podcast host of the* Burnt Creator *podcast, and my friend.*

I grew up with shame, deeply rooted from a young age as a pastor's kid. There was this expectation to be perfect, to excel in everything and to have no mind of your own – just follow whatever my dad, or rather God, said. It wasn't spoken but it was always there. I was the oldest and head-strong, and that only led to more clashes with my parents, who were both abusive in their own ways. I always felt like I wasn't who they needed me to be and that shame became my driving force.

Success, in many ways, became my attempt to earn their love. I thought that if I got rich, they would finally love me. But that never worked. I became obsessed with proving myself, thinking that if I had just stayed in church, led the worship team, maybe I'd have a better relationship with them. But now I realise I was just a child. I'm not responsible for how they receive me and I did everything I could.

Shame led me down some destructive paths. I started a company, I travelled the world, but I also spent money on things I didn't need. I convinced myself I was living my life but I was really just trying to prove something to my parents, trying to make them see me. It was heartbreaking to know that all my efforts, all my achievements, were rooted in trying to win their approval.

Watching myself on reality TV was a shock. It was like looking at a stranger, someone who thought they were living with peace but was actually engulfed in chaos. I didn't depend on anyone and no one depended on me. I was self-sufficient to a fault and it took a toll on my relationships. My body even forced me to get sick, to slow down, because I had to learn to lean on others.

The hardest lesson was learning to ask for help. I had always been the one people relied on but I didn't know how to ask for support when I needed it. This all traced back to my upbringing and never feeling safe to fail, never feeling loved regardless of success. That's the shame I carried into all my relationships.

It was like, 'Let me prove to you that I can be very, very successful and that God loves me and I love me, and everybody loves me.' That gets exhausting. It is not sustainable. This is not even who I am. And so, I don't think the show was a reflection of me.

Realising that was painful but necessary. It's crazy how shame can shape your entire life, how it can make you live a life that's not even yours. But the awareness, as hard as it is to face, is the first step to letting go and truly starting to heal.

That first week back after I finished filming the show was a fog of confusion and depression. I was blindsided by a profound identity crisis. Who was I if I wasn't the person

I had always thought myself to be? This wasn't just a momentary lapse; it was a year-long descent into a dark place. I'd always prided myself on knowing who I was, on being grounded in my sense of self. But here I was, adrift and lost. I questioned everything – my purpose, my worth, my place in the world.

Dating, of course, became another battleground for my insecurities. The pressure to fit into certain categories, to be the ideal partner, weighed heavily on me. Everyone wants to date someone successful, right? But what does that even mean? I found myself chasing after relationships in which I was trying to mould myself into something I wasn't, an image, a façade. I became hyper aware of how I didn't fit into the neat boxes that society tries to shove us into, and that made dating feel like an uphill battle.

I remember this one time on the show – it's all scripted in a sense, or at least structured – but there was this date with a woman who pushed all the wrong buttons. She had this demeanour that just rubbed me up the wrong way, and it was only our second date. She questioned my identity in a way that felt like a personal attack and, before I knew it, I was crying on national television, grappling with a flood of emotions I didn't even know I had. That moment wasn't planned, wasn't something I had prepared for, and it caught me off guard. But it also opened the floodgates.

There's something oddly liberating about being in a space where you're so exhausted, so stripped of your defences, that the truth just spills out before you can censor it. I've always believed that self-compassion is like revenge against shame; it's about getting the truth out before shame can tighten its grip.

The thing about the show is that it forced me to confront parts of myself that I had kept hidden, even from myself. When I started crying that day, it wasn't just about what the woman on the date had said. It was about this deep, underlying question that had been gnawing at me:

Who am I to the world?

I used to pride myself on not caring what others thought of me, but that day shattered that illusion.

For so long, I was running on empty, going through the motions and ignoring the parts of myself that needed attention. I was over-sharing with strangers on the show, which meant that people knew things about me that my closest friends didn't. It felt bizarre to be so vulnerable with people I barely knew but there was also a strange comfort in it. Maybe it's because you know you're only going to be in each other's lives for a short time, so it feels safer to let it all out.

After the show, everything changed. I started to realise that I didn't have to carry the weight of my shame alone. I didn't have to be perfect or have it all figured out to be worthy of love and connection. I began to see that it was okay – no, it was *necessary* to let people in, to let them help me carry the load. And in doing so, I found a freedom I hadn't known before. There were no more secrets, no more parts of myself that I was hiding from the world.

I think this is really valuable in so many ways for so many people. Not many people have had the sort of experience that I did on reality TV and, frankly, it's incredible that you can use that as a reframe. I guess people can sometimes look back on something, like a job they did or a presentation they feel bad about, and reflect back and maybe not feel great when thinking about that version of themself.

Obviously, they edited the show and they pulled out bits they wanted to for entertainment. But even so, I can still see how much I've grown. It's almost like being given a window into . . . not quite your inner child, but a younger version of yourself.

This new understanding transformed my relationships. The ones that were meant to last became stronger, while others naturally faded away. I learned to let go of the need to please everyone, to be everything to everyone. I stopped responding to every message, stopped engaging in small talk with people who no longer served a purpose in my life. It wasn't about being mean or uncaring; it was about self-preservation.

And then there was my relationship with my partner, the person who stood by me through it all. She was the one who showed me what it truly meant to be loved unconditionally. When I lost everything – my job, my home, my sense of self – she was there, not just as a shoulder to cry on but as someone who actively helped me rebuild.

It was hard for me to accept her help at first. I was so used to being the provider, the independent one. But she taught me that it's okay to lean on someone, that it doesn't make me weak or 'less than'.

My journey through shame was painful but it was also the most transformative experience of my life. It stripped away all the layers I had built up to protect myself and forced me to confront my deepest fears. In the end, it brought me to a place of peace, of acceptance and of genuine connection with the people who matter most. And for that, I am deeply grateful.

HOW WE SURVIVE

There is no woman I have met who cannot survive the events of her life, no matter how momentous and painful. However, I have never met a woman who does not suffer greatly from denying her own needs.

What I have learned to be true is this: shoving things down and compressing them into your system like a garbage compactor does not make them go away. Healing is never entirely done. Long-forgotten files pop up like the iPhone photo memories and can be triggering, surprising, shocking and revelatory, often in equal measure. But we can get to a place where we know that, whatever comes up, we have the capacity to resolve it.

For too long we have been shackled by the lies that shame whispered in our ears, keeping us trapped and small. We've been told to shrink ourselves, to conform to someone else's idea of who we should be. We have all at various points been pinned down by the weight of all we as women are made to carry. But no more. It's time to reclaim our power and live authentically, without apology or hesitation.

To live unapologetically is a rallying cry for rebellion, a call to arms for all those who refuse to be defined by the limitations of shame. For in the freedom of authenticity lies the power to transform not only your own life but the world around you. This is where we reclaim our sovereignty, where we become the phoenix rising from the ashes. It's a metamorphosis that happens within us, often unseen, but it is real and it is powerful.

Radical acceptance isn't passive; it's not throwing up your hands and resigning yourself to fate. It's the opposite. It's standing firm, staring directly into the chaos and choosing to believe that it's all happening *for* you, not *to* you. The universe makes no mistakes, and it has placed us here, in this moment, for a reason.

I used to believe in coincidences, random, meaningless events that bumped into each other, leaving us to make sense of the wreckage. I walked through life as if I were in a fog, stumbling over fragments of myself, unsure of where they fitted. I feared endings, I attempted to control outcomes and limit perceived losses, thinking that this was how I would keep myself safe. But now I know better. Every moment, every encounter, every heartbreak is a meticulously crafted piece of a much larger puzzle. It wasn't until I embraced radical acceptance that the fog lifted, revealing the masterpiece that had been forming all along.

My burnout was the best thing that could have happened to me. It forced me to the floor so as to be able to see the next step on the path leading me towards my destiny. My violent childhood gave me the ability to sit in pain with others. It contributes to living my purpose every single day, where I'm helping others to realise their full identity and full potential, helping them to move out from under the shadow of shame and trauma. Every time I 'lost' autonomy over my body, it helped me to understand how it feels when it has been snatched from another. Every heartbreak, duplicity, betrayal and moment of *Schadenfreude* that tore a hole in my life has helped shape my soul family, which now surrounds me.

I would not change a single thing. I truly believe that my life is beginning as it was always meant to, right now. I am the happiest, healthiest, sexiest, most excited that I have ever been. Every single thing, especially the people I have in my life now, is beyond what I once thought could be possible. I started with no plan, no knowledge of how good I could feel, but something inside me carried me here.

Now that I live without shame it feels like all of the light has been let in. For there is nothing that I pray you won't ask me about, no subjects that I dread being raised at the dinner table, no darting, awkward conspiratorial looks and silences that follow. No sticking my nails into my palms to stop the tears ready to spring forth at any moment. No clawing at my face, because the mask has long ago fallen away.

I refuse to bow to the expectations of a society that values compliance over courage and I no longer tolerate sanctimony from those who are not in service of others.

I will not apologise for being who I am, for wanting what I want, for living my life on my own terms. I am a wild woman and I am free.

This is the lesson we must learn: to be present, to be ourselves, to be unapologetically alive in a world that constantly tells us to be anything but.

I find solace in these words below by Clarissa Pinkola Estés. In these transitions, between sleep and awake in the stillness and the silence, we find our unapologetic selves. Like our ancestors long before us, they are calling us back to our own rewilding.

'BONE BY BONE, HAIR BY HAIR, WILD WOMAN COMES BACK. THROUGH NIGHT DREAMS, THROUGH EVENTS HALF UNDERSTOOD AND HALF REMEMBERED.'

— CLARISSA PINKOLA ESTÉS, *WOMEN WHO RUN WITH THE WOLVES*

MANIFESTO

We grow up hearing tales
Where no wild women prevailed
Slut, bitch, whore, witch
This is no life
Please people instead
Be a good girl, make your bed
Maybe one day you can be a 'perfect' wife
Shame made sure we 'knew our place'
Never took up too much space
No harm done?
And to think you almost won
I overheard shame one day
That's how I cleared it away
How you scolded our souls
With the lies that we are told
Only winning when we are dimming
Well no more
Shame spoke this to me
You must be the one to offer apology
Enough of these lies
Pull shame's veil from your eyes
Did you feel those bridges burn
As you allowed these pages to turn?
Listen as we rise in unison
Well, sorry, not sorry

I am so fucking tired of handing you my autonomy
No more my friend
I no longer bend
So the line below is where I offer my last sorry
To the only person who deserves this apology
Me

Sign here . . .
Your name
I am unapologetic

EPILOGUE

'Do not let too good to be true become the undoing of me and you.'

I did all of the work, or so I told myself. I learned the difference between feeling lonely and being happy alone with myself – or, rather, never to fear the latter again. I believed that I would be okay no matter what and, as the challenges prevailed, I kept showing up for myself and my daughter in a way that I hadn't before.

I stopped forcing events, actions or decisions, and things started to happen. Glimmers, momentum, opportunities.

I also allowed myself to lose some connections, by not breathing energy into them anymore. Not to make anyone right or wrong but as another exercise in relinquishing the control that had once given me a false sense of security. When some friend, romantic interest or work opportunity was swept off my path seemingly without warning I started to smile, knowing that, as it had now been proven time and time again, with every apparent 'loss' almost immediately came a new and much better 'gain'.

I learned that when I was acting in service, perfecting my craft and my technique of working with deep trauma, not only did my clients feel better, but so did I. With every person who shared their shame and pain with me, as I watched them leave our sessions cradling hope and self-compassion, I could no longer hear the naysayers.

My relationship with my daughter, the single person who showed me what it means to have family, flourished.

I needed less. Yet, I found myself with so much more. And I would tell everyone how content I was.

I did have everything that I wanted, except in one area of my life.

It was not love at first sight. But my soul recognised something in him instantly. We had arrived at the same place, at the perfect time, both a little battle-weary. Sometimes a little wounded and wary. Sometimes thinking, *This seems too good to be true.*

But there we were, ready to pick something up that felt like it had been waiting there for us. The soul's path, the master plan.

Meeting him was like coming home to a place I had never been before but had somehow always known existed. There was a sensation of peace from the moment that I met him.

That's not how I 'knew' he was the one.

That is how I knew that I was done.

This was the universe winking at me and saying, 'You have passed the tests and now you can take your rest.'

There's a profound beauty in shedding the masks we wear, in stripping away the layers of self-doubt and fear that have been built up over a lifetime. As I look back on my journey, I see how every step, every lesson and every struggle brought me closer to where I was meant to be.

At times things have not been without challenge or complication, but that is life, and life will continue to happen.

If I could go back to when I was begging the universe to just cut me a break after yet another disappointment or setback, seemingly in all areas of my life, I would want to tell myself this: never settle, never be less, never apologise for what sets your soul ablaze.

I had to become unapologetic in order to shed all of the old layers of shame that kept me from truly being available for a relationship. That is when it happens.

He is everything that I ever wished for in a partner. There has been no compromise on either side. He can hold me and all of my wild and has never once tried to tame me or push any shame on me.

If I had gone for anything before him I would have been settling for scraps.

I would have owed myself another apology.

ACKNOWLEDGEMENTS

For every single person who has been part of this book, whose words fill the pages alongside my own. Thank you for also seeing that this was something greater than ourselves and courageously sharing your stories and expertise with the world.

I know that each one of you share my passion to help another out of pain, even if that has meant re-living your own.

I have never believed that *Unapologetic* was mine, its purpose was always to reach those in need and become their friend in a time of crisis.

At times throughout this process I have been the one in crisis and have been lucky enough to receive the support of friends old and new.

Abigail Bergstrom, the finest literary agent, the most bewitchingly beautiful woman and formidable force. You have kept me together. I dreamed of being surrounded by fierce, fabulous, talented women and you embody all of these qualities – thank you, I adore you.

Susannah Otter, thank you for advocating for me, for this book, and for seeing the diamond within the rough. Niamh Anderson and Helena Fouracre for taking *Unapologetic* where she needed to be and always wearing hints of leopard print! Naomi Morris Omori for holding everyone together, a difficult task seemingly done with ease.

Friends become family and I am beyond grateful for all

of those that have taken that role within mine and Amber's life. With special thanks to those who have celebrated each step the dream, the writing and the publicity, Kirsty, Sarah and Lizzie.

Liz Marvin, you have helped me transform my own trauma into art. This became a 'book' before my eyes thanks to your passion for this project and the dance that you expertly led us through. The universe made no mistake when it put you on my path, I am eternally grateful for you.

Amanda Harkness and Morgan Amer from Hachette US, I have never had to explain myself or the book: you have seen me, this vision, and backed me from day one. I am so grateful for your energy, dedication, tenacity, friendship, for agreeing to the bats and wearing the company uniform of black to our meetings – I adore you both.

Karolina Kaim for helping me find the name for this book and the belief that I could do it.

Georgia Smith, thank you for not only backing me and this book long before there was any kind of 'brand' but also for protecting me and *Unapologetic* from those that do not align. May the only thing we ever 'sell out' be copies of this book.

John Richardson, thank you for keeping me stable through all of the storms of my own psyche whilst undertaking this process and for your help uncovering and unpacking a lot of my own 'stuff' that you knew I would face. You held that space for me when it rose its head time and again. I love your books, your guidance and help, but most of all Amber and I love you, Paula and your family, which has become part of our own. May you always help us put the fairy on our tree – in every sense.

Ruth Jones, thank you for your wisdom, mentorship and counsel, and for opening your heart and home to Amber and myself. Your kindness is something that I will never forget.

Alex, thank you for reading, reassuring and loving me through every draft, every doubt. You are my greatest support and the most beautiful soul that I know. I am proud and honoured to love you. I am excited for both of our sequels.

Amber, thank you, for giving me family, opening my heart, inspiring me every day in all that you are. Thank you for showing me the depth of unconditional love. I love you more than anything in this world and I always will.

Friends become family and I am beyond grateful for all of those who have taken that role within mine and Amber's life.

The greatest thanks of all goes to Nathalie Jones, without whom this book would never have been possible nor plausible.

We have shared memes, ideas, margs, tears, beds and so many laughs along what has been a truly home-made operation.

I have always maintained that you are 'too good' for me and now I hope that the whole world, including you, will see what artistry you have created, far beyond this beautiful cover and perfect aesthetic for the book, the brand and the business. I am excited to watch you soar – Amber and I love you so much.

REFERENCES

P. 19: C. G. Jung, *Nietzsche's Zarathustra: Notes of the Seminars given in 1934–1939 by C.G. Jung* (London, Routledge, 1989). P. 27: *Cambridge Academic Content Dictionary* © Cambridge University Press (web). P. 27: Mark Hyman, *The Dr. Hyman Show,* Episode 599: 'How trauma makes us sick and how we can hear with Gabor Maté'. P. 35: Brené Brown, *The Gift of Imperfection* (London: Hazelden Firm, 2010). P. 47: Sharon Blackie, *If Women Rose Rooted,* (London: September Publishing, 2016). P. 53: Pia Granjon speaking to Annalie Howling. P. 59: Cara speaking to Annalie Howling. P. 67: Leo Tolstoy, *Anna Karenina* (1878). P. 78: Bessel van der Kolk, *The Body Keeps the Score* (London: Penguin Books, 2014). P. 90: Madonna, as quoted in *The Independent,* 'Madonna: 20 of the best quotes from the Queen of Pop', 29 June 2023 (web). P. 106: Emily Ratajkowski, *My Body,* (London: Quercus, 2021). P. 112: Madeleine Albright, as quoted in the *Huffington Post,* 'Madeleine Albright: An Exclusive Interview', 6 December 2014 (web). P. 118: Phoebe Waller-Bridge, *Fleabag,* Series 2, Episode 3. Dir. by: Harry Bradbeer, London: BBC3. P. 136: Anna Salter, *Predators: Pedophiles, Rapists, and Other Sex Offender* (London: Basic Books, 2003). P. 148: Shonda Rhimes, *Year of Yes* (New York: Simon & Schuster and Marysue Rucci Books, 2015). P. 174: Brené Brown speaking to *The School of Greatness* podcast by Lewis Howes, Episode 899, 'Brené Brown: Create True Belonging and Heal the World.' P. 186: Michelle Obama speaking to the Young African Women Leaders Forum, Regina Mundi Church in Soweto, South Africa, 22 June 2011. P. 201: Clarissa Pinkola Estés, *Women Who Run with the Wolves* (London: Rider, 1992).